A COWBOY Never LIES

Dan Burnett

NEW WEST PRESS

Hamilton, Washington

A COWBOY NEVER LIES

Copyright © 1996 by Dan Burnett

ISBN: 0-9652375-0-8

Library of Congress Catalog Card Number: 96-092293

Publisher: New West Press/Hamilton, Washington

Photography: *Front Cover* — Portrait by Annette Medford
Back Cover — Bull rider Burnett in perfect form. *(Rodeo Photographer Unknown)*

Book Design: A2Z Graphics/Sedro-Woolley, Washington

Editor: Diane Freethy

Permission has been granted to use certain tradenames appearing throughout this book as follows:
Coors (Coors Brewing Company)
Del Monte (Del Monte Foods)
Stetson (John B. Stetson Company)
Tony Lama (Justin Industries, Inc.)

ATTENTION CORPORATIONS AND ORGANIZATIONS!
Quantity discounts are available for bulk purchases of this book for premiums, fundraisers or gift giving. For information, contact:
Marketing Department
New West Press
PO Box 32, Hamilton, WA 98255
360/826-4130.

PRINTED IN THE UNITED STATES OF AMERICA

Table of Contents

Acknowledgments

I gratefully acknowledge . . .

☆ My good buddy WAYNE GREENOUGH for encouraging me to write this book, and for his constant support and thoughtful reading of my manuscript.

☆ DIANE FREETHY for her skillful editing, expert typesetting, sound advice and comic relief.

☆ ALYSON HANSTEAD, JUDY HALL and ROSETTA SANZ for their early reading and critiques of my book.

☆ ANNETTE MEDFORD for her exceptional photography.

☆ And, last but not least, my wife for her patience, understanding and support.

Introduction

They say all things come full circle. When I was only three or four years old sometimes my Ma would ask me a question like:

"Did you throw rocks at the hens?"

I'd close my eyes and say:

"No Ma. Lady did, though."

Lady was my collie dog.

"You know, Dan, I can tell when you're telling me a story because you always close your eyes."

Well, I showed my Ma. I started telling my stories with my eyes open and I have been ever since.

Telling a story is what mothers call children's lies which are too innocent to cause any real trouble. There are four kinds of lies: storytelling, fibs, white lies and bold-faced lies, storytelling being the least serious offense. Stories are generally about ninety percent true, too. I admitted that rocks had been thrown at the hens. I just forgot which one of us did it.

The second kind of lie is a fib which is usually also told by children. A fib is told with the knowledge that your Ma and Pa, and most other adults, will probably see though it anyway. It's a half-hearted lie, a sort of test to see how smart adults really are. For instance, when my Pa would come back from town and see his calves panting, wet, huddled in a corner of the pen, and me and my cousin Fred each with a rope in our hand, he'd ask:

"Did you boys ride them calves while I was gone?"

"No, Pa."

The whipping that followed was a clear indication that we were the ones who failed the test.

The third kind of lie is a white lie. A white lie is a bold-faced lie told as a kindness to someone else. It isn't the truth, but its purpose is to prevent hurting someone's feelings, like when my wife cooks a new dish and asks:

"Honey do you like it?"

"Boy do I! But you know, I just remembered I forgot to pick up feed. I have to run into town real quick. I'll be right back."

After I pick up the feed I drive through McDonald's on the way home. When I get back she apologizes because the food is too cold to eat, and I tell her:

"That's okay, Honey. I've had plenty."

And she thinks I'm a helluva nice guy.

The fourth kind of lie is a plain brown bag, generic, straight-forward, total fabrication called a bold-faced lie. It needs no further explanation and, just for the record, I reserve those exclusively for emergencies like when I'm in trouble with my wife.

As long as I can remember, people have been telling me I should write a book about the stories I've told them. So, I decided to do just that. This book contains ten of those stories about the almost absolutely true adventures of me and my rodeo buddies. I had to change some names and places to protect the innocent, if in fact there are any. That accounts for the four white lies. There are also two fibs, which I'll let you figure out for yourself. However, there aren't any bold-faced lies because, as I mentioned, I reserve those for real emergencies. Which reminds me, there's something I need to tell my wife.

6

"No, Honey, I did not cash in my life insurance policy to get this book printed."

Just so there are no misunderstandings, all cowboys are not alike. The Professional Rodeo Cowboys Association (PRCA) was first known as RCA (Rodeo Cowboys Association). And before high octane, high performance athletes, there were old-fashioned, hell-raising cowboys like me and my buddies. The addition of the word "professional" was not without purpose and intention. The powers-that-be decided that cowboys needed a new image. I'm here to tell you, they not only got their new image, they got a new breed of cowboy to go with it.

I'll confess, most of us on the circuit during the fifties and sixties had notorious reputations, and a description of our behavior would have included an interesting vocabulary. But it would not have included the word "professional." Now, that isn't because we didn't earn our living (meager as it was) from rodeo, or because we weren't damn good at what we did. No, it was because of the manner in which we pursued our craft.

We were young, tireless and had an unsatiable passion for life and every experience we could chase, corral or capture. We rode everything with hair, drank from every watering hole, and cut every filly out of the herd that we could, because . . . well, because we could, I guess.

A lot of folks would like to forget some of us ever existed. And a few folks have tried, which is why you haven't read about us before, or seen our pictures in the Rodeo Hall of Fame. It's not that we're not famous in our own right. It's just that what got us famous is considered out of style in today's sophisticated society.

I'll be the first to admit that we lacked the professional attitude and manners that have made the PRCA boys so popular today. Now, I'm not saying that's bad or good. I'm just saying the way things are today don't sound like any fun to me at all. I remember the good times and the old boys who lived them. It's only right that they should be remembered. True enough, about ninety percent of the guys I used to run with are dead now, which brings me to another point. There aren't many of us left, and I hate to brag, but I always did tell the best stories, so it's only right I should be the one to tell these.

Me and my buddies rodeoed for a lot of reasons, but money wasn't one of them. The PRCA boys today make more in one show than all of us put together made in a year. It wasn't for fame either. Rodeos weren't nationally televised or videoed, and rarely attended by anyone but the cowboys themselves, and the locals who lived nearby the rodeo grounds. You literally had to be there to experience it. The only way we got any recognition was by one cowboy telling another cowboy behind the chutes, by bartenders telling bankers, by farmers telling ranchers, by a few girls telling all the other girls, or by me telling anybody who'd listen.

We didn't do it for glamour or glory. We didn't have sponsors, crash helmets, flak-jackets, personal trainers or custom-made rigs. If we were lucky, we had a loan from a buddy drunk enough to be congenial, a starched white shirt and a clean pair of Wrangler jeans, a volunteer ambulance driver, and a beat-up old pickup.

We didn't do it for the fans either, although we sure liked the applause. We did it for fun, adventure and the dance. Bob Wills was king back then, and any man who could two-step was almost as popular as a cowboy who made the whistle. If you could do both, you could pretty much pick any filly from the herd. Now, if you've never heard ole Bob play then you've never been to a real dance. When he started up, he never stopped except for the boys to make a pit stop. Brother, you had better come to dance when Bob Wills was playing. A sweet-smelling woman who melts in your arms and Bob Wills playing a two-step . . . well, it just doesn't get any better than that.

And another reason we rodeoed — we did it to keep from doing something distasteful like getting a real job. We knew that dreaded day would come soon enough and we weren't about to hurry it along.

I feel sorry for any man who's never had a chance to rip and run with his buddies. There's been a lot of talk about this male bonding thing, and I believe in it. You're supposed to trust another man enough to tell him your feelings, and do man things together. But that ain't nothing new. When you sleep eight to a room, scrape mold off what's left of a pound of bologna, slap it between two slices of stale bread and then all take a bite; if six of you share one bottle of aftershave; if you're willing to sit on another cowboy's lap in an over-crowded truck to get to a rodeo, and you trust another ole boy to pull your bull rope . . . now that's male bonding.

Male bonding ain't for everybody, though. Take Jerry for instance. He was a good ole boy but he just wasn't cut out for the kind of intimacy us cowboys were used to. Buzz and Delbert didn't quite get the hang of it either. We weren't all cut out to be cowboys, but we all went along for the ride just the same.

9

Dedication

This book is dedicated to all the old cowboys of the Rodeo Cowboy Association, to members of the old Cowboy Turtle Association, and to Billy Weeks, a true cowboy who had more "try" than any other I ever met.

NIGHTMARE IN WICKENBURG

I was at home on the high plains of New Mexico. It was hot and dry as usual and I was bored out of my skull, just sitting there on the porch, looking at nothing because there was nothing to look at. I always said that old country was so flat that if you stood up and stared real hard you could see the back of your head. Anyway, when the phone rang I darn near busted my neck trying to get to it. It was my buddy Levi.

"Hey there, Hoss. You all busy out there?"

Hoss was my nickname. I think people started calling me that back when Bonanza was popular on TV, but I'm not really sure why. I didn't look anything like Dan Blocker, even if we did have the same first name. I was so tall and skinny that if I drank a red soda pop and turned sideways I looked like a thermometer.

"Yep, I'm pretty busy. Maybe I better call you back later."

Levi laughed. He knew the only thing I'd be busy doing was sleeping. At that time, besides sleeping and eating, I did one thing and one thing only . . . rodeo. I'm sure he was surprised I even answered the phone.

"What do you say we go to the rodeo in Wickenburg?"

"I don't have enough money for a can of Copenhagen, let alone drive six hundred miles to a rodeo. That last show left me and my butt both busted."

"That's why we need to go. It's a good show and easy money. It's a cinch, Hoss! Besides, there's always a big party."

11

"Let me think on it a bit and I'll call you back."

I started wracking my brain trying to think who I might borrow some money from, but I'd tapped every resource I could think of. Then I got an idea. All I needed was somebody to back me for half my winnings. That's when I thought about Fred, one of the local bootleggers outside of town.

I thought it was ironic that anyone who liked to party as much as I did lived in the only dry county in the state. There were plenty of bootleggers, though — so many of them they had to wear signs around their necks to keep from selling hooch to each other.

I loaded up and headed out to Fred's, to see if he had any money, hoping at least to get a free cold one. When I got there, Fred was talking to this older feller. The man was short and skinny. He had some hair, but not much. He'd let it grow long on the left side, long enough to comb over the top and flop down on the right side. He wore thick, wire-rimmed spectacles like the ones people have to wear when they read too much. I think this ole boy was from town because his polyester pants were just short of the top of his loafers, exposing his white socks.

"Hoss, this here is Jerry."

We shook hands and Fred offered me a beer. The three of us shot the shit for awhile, then I hit Fred up for some money. Fred said he was sorry but business hadn't been so good lately . . . "too much competition, I guess."

"Well, that's too bad. You were my last hope, Fred."

"What about finding a sponsor?"

"That's not a bad idea, Fred."

Jerry was real interested in our conversation.

"What do you mean, a sponsor?" he asked.

12

"Sometimes these ole boys, like Dan here, find a guy to put up the entry fee, and if the cowboy wins he gives half to his sponsor. You know how cowboys are. They'll do anything to get to a show. Ain't that right, Hoss?"

"Yep, just about anything. I even went out with one of my sister's friends once just so I could borrow money from her."

Jerry sat quietly drinking his beer for a few minutes. Then he stood up, emptied what was left in his bottle with one swig, and tossed it into the metal trash can.

"You know, I've been a school teacher might near all my life. I've never done much else and never been to Arizona. I think I might like to see that country. What do you think?"

Fred spoke up before I got a chance.

"Well, you'd sure enough see the country. It's about six hundred miles over there, and chances are you're gonna make some money 'cause ole Dan here stands as good a chance of winning as anybody. He's sure enough a good hand, but I gotta warn you. He'll want to take Levi, and those two are real trouble. They can cover some mean stock but they drink hard and party long. It ain't no use tyring to get him to leave his buddy behind either. That's just the way cowboys are. Do you think you're up to it?"

I interrupted.

"Why, Fred. I never knew you thought so highly of me and Levi."

Jerry opened another beer. He walked slowly away from us, then spun around on his heels and said:

"I've lived a boring, uneventful life for darn near

13

sixty years. If I don't do something I really want to do now, I might not ever do it."

"Atta boy, Jerry!" I said, slapping him on the back. Jerry was plum excited about our deal.

"Hell, I'll even pay for the gas!"

He took a deep breath, threw his shoulders back, his chest out, and strutted up to Fred.

"Now don't you worry none about me, Fred. I've been waiting for a chance like this all my life."

Fred shook his head. He'd been down the road with me and Levi himself a couple of times, and that was about all he could stand.

I didn't give Jerry a chance to change his mind.

"Partner, I'm going to the house to call Levi and pack my gear. I'll meet you back here in exactly one hour."

I didn't waste any time calling Levi.

"Hey, I found a sponsor. He's going with us, and the best part is, he's paying for the gas. So you can go ahead and buy some whiskey with your money."

"Okay! I'll be ready to go as soon as you get here."

I picked Jerry up first. He looked a little surprised when he saw my old pickup.

"Are you sure three of us will fit in here?"

He pushed a "dead soldier" (that's cowboy for empty whiskey bottle) on the floor and shoved my war bag over toward the driver's seat.

"Three? No sweat! I've stacked them five deep and still had room for the cooler. Throw your suitcase in the back. As soon as we get to Levi's I'll put my gear in the back, too."

Jerry got in and I peeled out down the gravel road towards Levi's place. When we pulled up, Levi came sailing out the front door with his war bag and a half gallon of liquor. The bottle looked familiar.

"Did you get that out at Fred's place?" Jerry asked.

"Yeah, it's rotgut all right. It'll melt your feathers, get you drunk and turn you crazy. Fills you right up, too. A few pulls on this jug and you couldn't eat if you had to. That ought to cut down on some expenses."

Jerry already was looking a little nervous. He slid down in the seat and stared straight ahead. I hopped out and threw my war bag in the back with Levi's, then the two of us got in the cab with Jerry sandwiched between us. Levi handed him the jug. He took a sip, but he could barely swallow. He passed it to me and I passed it back to Levi. Jerry did his best to keep up with us, trying his darnedest to be a good sport, but he came down with a bad case of heartburn or something. After every swig, he'd hit his chest with his fist and grunt like a hog.

About a hundred miles down the road Jerry saw a bar out there in the middle of nowhere.

"Say, boys, if you'll pull off at that watering hole, I'll buy us all some beer. I just can't handle that jug of yours. I think my teeth are getting loose."

That suited us just fine. I shut her down right in front of the bar. Now, everything might have been okay except for one small complication. We no sooner sat down than I spotted a guy I really didn't want to run into. I had been a little too friendly with this ole boy's wife in the past. It wasn't really my fault. She told me her old man was a cripple and never paid her no attention anymore. I believed her, too . . . until I heard a truck drive up about three in the morning and watched her crippled husband jump out the driver's seat and come stomping in the house. I barely got away with my hide.

I hoped maybe he was too drunk to recognize me, but he did.

"You son-of-a-bitch!" he hollered as he threw his beer bottle at me.

I ducked just in time, but the bottle hit ole Jerry in the head, knocking him clean out of his chair.

The fight was on. Me and Levi jumped up and the old boy and two of his friends met us at the table just a-swinging. Jerry was still on the floor and all five of us were walking on him like he wasn't there. Every time he tried to get up somebody would knock him down again. The ole boy and his friends had been in the bar since morning, so we made short work of them, but poor Jerry was really the worse for wear. He hadn't even thrown a punch and his shirt was tore half off. He had a big knot on his head where the bottle hit him and he was missing some hide from his chin, too. His eyes were big as saucers and he could barely stand up. He had never even seen a real barroom brawl, let alone be caught in the middle of one. But he managed to stagger to the bar and ordered a case of beer to go. That's when the bar owner started cussing me. His timing was real bad. I reached across the bar, drug him over it and proceeded to whip his butt.

"I'm going to let you up," I said when I realized I was in control of the situation. "Get our beer and we'll be out of here."

Dazed, the man followed my instruction, and we left. But just as I opened the door of the pickup, gunfire hit the mirror and glass flew everywhere. He was standing in the doorway shooting at us. With Levi and Jerry fast behind, I dove into the front seat, and we tore out of the

16

parking lot, throwing gravel in every direction.

Me and Levi were laughing and carrying on as soon as we got out to the road. You'd have thought this was an everyday occurrence. And actually, it wasn't all that uncommon. Jerry popped the top on a can of beer and started sucking it down. He was still a little stunned.

"Damn, boys! We haven't even been on the road three hours. I expected to see some Arizona backroads and a good rodeo. I didn't know this trip was going to include gunfire. I'll be lucky to make it home alive."

"Don't worry about anything, Jerry," I reassured him. "There's no extra charge for gunfights . . . or girls."

I drove straight through the night to get to the rodeo on time. My driving got a little slower as I got drunker, and Jerry offered to take the wheel once or twice. But seeing how he didn't know the roads like I did, I decided I could do the job okay. Jerry was so nervous I was sure he'd stay awake, but both of us kept dozing off, and Levi was out cold. Must have been those lullabies I sang. I always liked to sing when I was sleepy but my version of *Tiger by the Tail* kept everybody awake — everybody but Levi, that is.

We got to Wickenburg the next morning and had a few hours to kill before the rodeo started at one o'clock. Jerry was so tired he couldn't wiggle so he just sat in the truck while Levi and me went and found the water trough in the catch pen to wash off some of the blood and beer. We were raring to go. But cowboys have their priorities, too. After paying our entry fees we started looking around the stands for some girls to take to the dance after the rodeo. I spotted a gal I knew and another older woman. Now, Carol Fay was a good-looking gal but her

17

friend looked like she'd been rode hard and put away wet. She had bulges where bulges weren't supposed to be, and her hot-pink stretch pants outlined every one of them. Her tank top was so tight her freckled cleavage spilled over the top of it, and I swear she'd put her makeup on with a putty knife. Some of her sparkling blue eye shadow had flaked off her eyelids and was sticking to the pound-and-a-half of foundation which ran plum into her hairline. Her eyebrows had been shaved off, and she must've been shaking that morning when she drew them back on, because one extended almost to the top of her left ear. Apparently, she didn't mind spending money on lipstick, either. She was wearing nothing short of a full tube. Her hair was frozen stiff with spray — big and tall enough to expose a couple inches of black roots under the silver blonde.

"Hi Dan. I was sure hoping you'd be here this weekend. This is my mom, Laverne."

Her mother gave me the once-over.

"You're right honey. He is pretty cute. Are there any more at home like you?"

"As a matter of fact, I brought a buddy with me, and we're both looking for dates for the dance tonight."

"Look no farther, cowboy," Carol Fay said as she slid her arm under mine."

"So, where's my hot date?" Laverne asked.

"He's waiting for us in my pickup."

All in all I probably could have done better for Jerry, but it was a package deal. Besides, I knew he'd be too shy to round up his own woman. I headed back to the truck with both gals, one on each arm. I had to hold Laverne steady. I guess she'd hit the hooch pretty early, but she sure had a happy disposition, and she took a liking to

18

Jerry as soon as she saw him.

"Look here, Jerry. I got you a date for the dance tonight. This here is Laverne."

I was so proud of myself for finding Jerry a partner that I missed the look of horror on his face when Laverne let out a squeal.

"Oh Honey, you're so cute!"

She jumped in the truck beside him, removed the cigarette from the corner of her mouth and laid a big wet kiss on poor ole Jerry. When she let him go, that red lipstick was spread from her nose to her chin, and Jerry looked like he was wearing war paint. He scrambled to the other side of the seat, gasping for air. I couldn't blame him. Laverne was so tanked that if he'd lit a match inside the cab, the whole thing would have gone up in flames.

Jerry tried to say something but nothing would come out. He was speechless. Laverne grabbed him by the collar, pulled him across the seat next to her and started singing *I'm in the Mood for Love*. That's when I decided to get out of there.

"Well, partner, I'm going to find out just what I drew. You two behave yourselves now, and don't do anything I wouldn't do."

"I don't know what in the hell that might be," Jerry mumbled as he looked Laverne in the face for the first time. "Excuse me ma'am, but I have to talk to this guy just a minute."

"Well, okay. But you hurry back, you little cutie."

She pinched him on the behind as he jumped out of the truck and grabbed my arm.

"Man," Jerry pleaded, "Don't leave me with that woman. "I'm begging you. She's all over me like a cheap suit. Did you see that vice grip she had on my thigh? I never heard anyone talk so much and so fast."

"Jerry, she wants you. What can I say? She seems like a nice enough gal. Besides, I'm rather partial to that daughter of hers."

I patted him on the back and headed for the arena where I found Levi. He had been watching us from a distance and was laughing his fool head off.

"Hoss, you're cold-blooded. I saw Jerry over there. It looked like he was begging for his life."

"You know, I think he was."

"I think he might have made an escape, though. While you two were talking Laverne staggered over to that red pickup to use the mirror to put some more war paint on. When Jerry saw she wasn't looking, he slipped behind the truck and headed for the stands. He was running and breathing so hard it looked like he might pass out."

"Where is he now? Do you see him?"

We scanned the stands, but Jerry was nowhere to be found. The grand entry was about to begin. Me and Levi faced the arena with our hats over our hearts. The flag passed by, and when the national anthem started to play, everyone stood up. That's when we spotted ole Jerry. And so did Laverne. From ground-level, as drunk as she was, she somehow managed to see him clear up at the top of the stands.

"There you are!" she screamed loud enough to drown out the *Star-Bangled Banner*. "You naughty, naughty boy! I thought you got lost."

Determined to sit next to her date, Laverne started climbing towards Jerry, literally crawling over the top of the crowd and rearranging hairdo's and hats as she went.

"Damn, Levi! Would you look at that? I think ole Jerry is going to jump."

He didn't. But I'll just bet he thought real hard on it. It was too late anyway. Laverne had made her way up the stands and had wedged herself in beside him. She put a grip on his arm that no living man could have broken. He was stuck.

"I made it, Sweetie," she yelled.

She laid another big kiss on his cheek. Her jug was sticking out of the white patent leather purse hanging around her neck.

"Sweetie, are you sure you wouldn't like a little drinky-poo?"

When he said no, she proceeded to drink it all herself, and then threw up on the people in front of them. Levi and me wondered if we should try to rescue Jerry, but decided he was able to take care of himself. When Laverne passed out a few minutes later, he made his getaway and caught up with us behind the chutes.

"There you two are. That's it! I've had it! Let's go home."

I tried to calm him down.

"Jerry, we can't go home. We haven't even been up yet."

"I don't care. My nerves are completely shot. I didn't sleep all night because every time I dozed off you did, too. You ran off the road just enough to throw gravel under the truck and skid around until I woke up. Didn't you notice me sticking to the roof of the truck like a cat?"

"Well, no, can't say that I did but . . ."

"No buts! I haven't eaten a thing except your cowboy pork chops. I'm telling you, beer is a beverage. It is not

21

one of the food groups."

"But Jerry, aren't you having a good time so far?"

"Hell no! The only thing I have to be grateful for is I think I finally lost that little honey you fixed me up with. That women is plain nuts. She's almost as crazy as you two!"

That's when Levi spoke up.

"Look, Jerry. Everything is going to be okay. I'm up in just a few minutes. Why don't you just relax and enjoy the rodeo."

Jerry knew he was defeated.

"I'm going to hide out somewhere and watch you two. But as soon as you're finished riding I want to go home."

We watched him slink off toward the stands.

"Levi, do you think he forgot the rodeo is two days?"

"I sure hope so, Hoss. We can spring that on him later. I just don't know if he's up to all this."

Levi was the third rider. He drew a horse called Poker Chip — a horse you could win some money on if the competition wasn't too tough. The first two guys up were local dudes. They lasted a couple of jumps and fell off. Then it was Levi's turn. He slid up on his rigging, shook his face and they jerked the gate open. Poker Chip baled out in a high dive, but Levi kept his spurs buried in his shoulders and got him marked out. Poker Chip had disqualified a lot of cowboys on the first jump. If both spurs aren't over the point on the shoulders the first jump out, the ride doesn't count. Levi was off to a good start.

The horse jumped and kicked plum over his and Levi's heads. Levi was knocking the hair off of him, pulling his knees to his ears. Damn! I liked to watch Levi ride.

22

If he was right, he could ride with the best of them. Four seconds out, Poker Chip started to weaken. He wasn't kicking half as high when the whistle blew. Levi got off on the pick-up man and headed back for the chutes when the announcer called out.

"That last ride was worth sixty-seven points, folks. Give him a hand. He's in the lead so far."

Levi kicked at the dirt and cussed.

"That weak-hearted son-of-a-bitch! He started out great, then faded to nothing."

"Oh, don't take it so hard, Levi. You're in the lead."

"Big damn deal! I'm the only one who's got a horse covered. If he had just kept firing like he started out, I'd have scored at least seventy-five, maybe more. Damn the luck!"

But luck was with Levi because everyone else was either bucked off or scored lower than he did. Levi was the winner that day.

Someone came up behind me and poked me in the ribs. It was Billy Weeks. He was an old hand who had been going down the road since 1949, which was unbelievable. Most cowboys weren't that tough. Rodeo is a brutal sport and few men ever lasted twenty years or more. Me and Levi had a lot of respect for Billy. He had helped both of us when we first started in the pro's. Billy had a big ornery grin on his face.

"Ah, just the two fools I've been looking for. The two fellas that were gonna help me in the wild horse race got so drunk they can't move. What would you boys say to helping me out?"

"Billy, why in the world did you enter the wild horse race?" I asked. "Do you have a death wish?"

23

"No, I don't. You know, you boys are missing out on a chance to pick up some easy money at these little shows. You ought to make more of them. The pay ain't bad, and your only competition is the local yokels who don't know a thing about riding rough stock."

I swear there wasn't another man living I would have gotten in the wild horse race for, but I couldn't refuse Billy.

"Sure," I said. "We'll do the mugging. It's been at least two or three hours since someone has tried to kill us. It's getting kind of boring, ain't it, Levi?"

Levi shook his head.

"Damn, Hoss, you get us into more scrapes. One of these days we'll be like ole Jerry — wondering if we're gonna get home alive. Oh well, it might be fun at that."

The wild horse race is not a regular rodeo event. Some shows include it because the crowd loves it. But most cowboys wouldn't enter if you held a gun on them. The object of the race is to get the wild horse stopped after he's been let out of the chute, in a halter with a twenty-foot rope attached. It takes all three men to stop the horse. Then one guy has to run from the end of the rope up to the horse's head, grab an ear and twist it until the animal stands still. The second man puts the saddle on, cinches it up and climbs on the horse. The mugger and the guy holding the rope let go once the rider is mounted. Whoever rides to the other end of the arena and crosses the line with his horse is the winner. That in itself is no easy job, even for three crazy cowboys. But that's not the wild part. The wild part comes when they turn out eight horses at the same time. That's when it gets, as the cowboys say, "western." Anyone who enters knows that he's gonna get

24

kicked, stomped and probably dragged at least once. So, that event is usually reserved for the local boys dumb enough to play cowboy for a day. I couldn't believe we were actually going out there with those other fools this time.

We found Billy right before the race, standing confidently in front of the chute with his saddle. We pulled our hats down low and positioned ourselves. The whistle blew, all the gates flew open and the wreck was on!

Eight horses bolted out of the chutes in a dead run. When they hit the ends of their ropes, some of them boys were jerked clean out of their Tony Lamas. The team next to us got knocked down and rolled up in a ball. They looked like a big knot — arms, legs and hats sticking out everywhere. One idiot had tied the rope around his waist. His horse hit the end of it so hard it jerked all three of them down at once. His buddies let go of the rope and the horse took off dragging him down the arena, bouncing like a rubber ball until he landed face first. Then he plowed up the arena with his chin while the horse circled back and ran right through the rest of us. The cowboys scattered every which way, unable to see through the thick cloud of dust. It was hard for us to stay with our teams and horses. With dirt flying, horses squealing and cowboys cussing, the fans who paid to see this wild rodeo were sure getting their money's worth.

We finally got our horse stopped. Levi jumped up to mug him and another horse ran over him. The rope caught Levi behind the knees and flipped him like a pancake. He must have heard Billy and me laughing at him because he came up cussing, got right back on that horse's head and eared him down. Billy was right on him, too. He had his saddle throwed on and was reaching under for the

25

girth when the horse cow-kicked him, knocking him to the ground. That bronc spun around, threw Levi off his head and stepped all over Billy with his front hooves. I hung onto that rope like a calf to a teat. I knew if that horse got away we couldn't win. Levi jumped back on the horse's head while Billy saddled him and stepped on. He put one hell of a ride on that bronc, but it wasn't enough to win the race. He still had to cross the line before someone else did.

The whistle blew and all Billy got for his effort was applause. He tried to step off that horse real easy but he landed head first like a sack of feed. We were brushing the dirt off our hats when he joined us back at the chutes.

"That was a great ride, Billy," I said. "But you could use a little work on your dismount."

He just grinned and offered to buy us both a drink down at the bar after the show.

Meanwhile, I began to wonder where Jerry had got to. I hadn't seen hide nor hair of him anywhere, but after the rodeo when we went back to the truck, he was right there waiting for us.

"How'd you like my ride, Jerry?" Levi asked.

"I just don't understand you two. How in the heck can you drive all that way without sleep, drink all that booze, get into a fight, get shot at, and still ride a bucking horse?"

Levi smiled.

"It's a dirty job but someone's got to do it."

"What I really couldn't believe is that wild horse race. How could anyone be crazy enough to get out there and try to kill himself like that?"

"I'll admit it's pretty glamorous, but it's not for everyone," I said.

"Well, I'm just glad it's over. All I want now is a hot meal and a soft bed."

About that time our dates showed up.

"Hi, boys. Are you ready?"

"Who are these women?" Jerry wanted to know.

"Jerry, ole buddy," I whispered, "These girls are our dates for the dance."

"What? Where's Laverne's daughter?"

"I don't know. I haven't seen her since the bull riding, so I asked Bobby Sue there and her friend to go with us."

Jerry leaned out the window of the pickup and looked around.

"What are you looking for?"

"Their mommas."

"You can relax. They came alone. But speaking of mommas, what happened to Laverne? I thought she took a real liking to you."

I probably shouldn't have said that. Now Jerry was mad again.

"I don't know what you two have up your sleeves now, but I want no part of it."

Levi and the girls were getting impatient.

"You ready to go to the party?" Levi hollered.

"No!" Jerry shouted. "I don't want to go to a party. I'm tired, I'm sore and I don't even know how you two are still breathing."

"Oh, that ain't no problem," I assured him. "Me and Levi do this all the time. Look, we'll miss you if you don't come to the party. I think you'd have a big old time. If you don't want to, that's okay, but you got to come and have one drink with us."

27

Jerry knew it was no use arguing. He got in the back of the truck so me and Levi and the girls could all fit up front. I felt like showing off a little, so I started turning wheelies in the parking lot. With the gals giggling and hanging on to Levi and me, that pickup slid around in the gravel like we were in an ice rink. When I turned around to take a look at Jerry, he had rolled across the bed of the truck and crashed feet first into the tailgate. Coughing and choking from the dust, he was frantically waving for me to stop. I couldn't see his face but I'm sure he wasn't smiling.

By the time the dust had cleared, I could see Jerry scowling — hard. Not wanting to push it, I straightened the wheel and pulled out onto the pavement. I floorboarded it down the road towards town and came to a screeching halt in the parking lot behind the bar. Poor Jerry went flying one more time. Levi and I jumped out and raced each other to the door, leaving Jerry and the girls behind. We were anxious to get on with the night's events and decided to announce our entrance with a big war whoop. Nobody noticed. We'd walked right into a fight. Three or four old boys were swinging at each other. They weren't doing a lot of damage, but it was enough to annoy a local dude who threw a full bottle of beer in their direction. Then a chair whizzed by Levi's head and crash-landed against the jukebox causing the needle to scream across the record. But ole Merle Haggard kept on a-singing, and the cowboys leaning on the bar kept on a-jawing like nothing unusual was happening. When I turned to see if the girls had followed us, I spotted Jerry standing there. He was blinking like he had something stuck in his eye.

"Jerry, what's the matter?"

"I was hoping I was dreaming and this was a nightmare. At least that way I know I'd eventually wake up back in the real world."

"Aw, come on, Jerry. We're going to have a good time tonight."

I gave him a little shove in the direction of the bar and he stumbled right into the path of a big cowboy with a bad disposition, knocking his drink out of his hand.

"I'm gonna tear your head off, you little . . ."

"Just hold on partner." I stepped between the two of them. "My buddy here was in such a hurry to get a drink he bumped into you. It was an accident. He didn't mean nothing by it. He'd like to buy you another round to make up for it."

The cowboy liked that idea okay, but Jerry was speechless. One thing was true: he was in a hurry to get that drink now. I ordered him a double and slapped him on the back as he polished it off.

"How do you like it so far, Jerry? You know, in a couple of hours this place will really get wild. That's when the fun will start."

He gave me the most painful look.

"What am I doing here? I don't belong here. These people are crazy. Everyone is drunk, or working on it real fast. The music is so loud my head hurts. I'm surrounded by people I know want to kill me. I . . . I . . . I . . ."

It was time for some wild west stories. Levi and me started telling the girls about the time we tried to run over a hitchhiker but missed and got his suitcase instead. The girls laughed. They laughed at everything we said no matter how ridiculous it was. But Jerry wasn't laughing. His knuckles were white from clinging so hard to his beer bottle, and he jumped when I hollered.

29

"Hey, Jerry! You need to loosen up a little. What you need is a woman and I'm just the man who can find you one."

Jerry had lost his voice from sheer nervousness, and there was a pleading look on his face. He shook his head violently.

I chuckled and said: "Well, maybe not. You didn't draw so good in the last round. You know, I need to talk to you about your taste in women. It looks like you need another beer, though."

Levi ordered another round. Three hours later we were still drinking and lying to each other when Bobby Sue suggested we drive to another dance back in Phoenix.

"It's too crowded in here to dance. Later on we can party at my house."

"That sounds good to me," I said, and Levi agreed.

Jerry wasn't making a sound, but all kinds of faces. We watched him for a minute and when he finally opened his mouth he yelled so loud, damn near everybody in the bar turned around to look.

"No, I can't do it. I can't go anymore. I've had it. Leave me here. Leave me in the truck. Take me out back and shoot me, but don't make me go to Phoenix."

Then he just started quivering all over. Levi looked at me kind of surprised. I put my arm around Jerry.

"It's okay, partner. You can stay in the truck if you want to."

We led him out to the pickup.

"There now, Jerry, you can stay right here. But we're gonna have to put all our stuff up here with you because if we don't somebody might steal it."

"Okay, okay! I dont care. That's fine."

We loaded our war bags, suitcases and saddles and everything else in the cab of the truck. We shoved it over as far as we could and Jerry got in on top and wallered out a little place to sit. It was impossible to lay down, but I'm sure he didn't care, just as long as he could stay there. I shut the door and took the keys with me. I was half afraid he might take off and leave us if I didn't.

"Partner, we'll see you later. Now, don't let nobody steal our stuff."

It was eleven o'clock the next day when me and Levi decided to go to breakfast. Levi opened the door of the truck.

"Where's Jerry?"

"What do you mean, where's Jerry? He couldn't have left. Where would he go?"

I took a look for myself. All I could see was a big stack of clothes and our gear piled up in the center of the seat.

"Damn Levi! What's that smell?"

I picked up a dirty sock and threw it at him.

"That's yours!"

He picked the sock off his shoulder and tossed it back on the floorboard. Then I threw a dirty t-shirt at him.

"Yours!"

I found another sock.

"Yours, too!"

When I pulled a pair of muddy jeans off the stack and tossed them out, he just threw them back on the floorboard.

"Now look," I said. "You're not leaving them smelly clothes in my truck."

Levi protested when I threw a pair of his under-shorts down on the ground.

"Phew! Those are yours, too. Why the hell did you bring all these damn dirty clothes with you, Levi?"

"Hell, you didn't give me any time to get ready at all. I'm wearing the only clean stuff I had."

"Well, you weren't going to wear this stuff later, were you?"

"No! What kind of slob do you think I am?"

"That's just what I'm trying to figure out?"

"I was going to wash them later."

"Right!"

A weak, shaky voice came from under the stack of smelly gear.

"Get me out of here."

"Oh my God, it's Jerry," I said.

I shoved the rest of the junk over and there he was all curled up in a little ball, shivering.

"Jerry, what are you doing under that stinky stuff?"

"I . . . I . . . I was freezing to death out here. I couldn't find anything else to cover up with."

I should have warned him that little old windbreaker of his was too thin for the cold desert nights. I drug him out from under the pile of ripe laundry. Even his polyester pants were crumpled up, and his hair was hanging down on the long side, almost to his shoulder, leaving the top of his head and the other side completely bare.

"Hell, Jerry," Levi sounded sympathetic. "Why didn't you call us to come and get you?"

"No thank you. I have no desire to be attacked by a bunch of crazy cowboys . . . or those wild women you've been running with."

"Let's get some breakfast," I said.

"I don't want any breakfast. I just want to go home. Take me home."

Levi was determined to change ole Jerry's mind.

"Now Jerry, some hot coffee will warm you up. Besides, Dan is riding in the rodeo today. You don't want to miss that, do you?"

"Yes! I can't stand it anymore. Leave me here and let me die."

"No sense in getting melodramatic about it, Jerry," I said. "Come on now."

Jerry could barely crawl out of the truck. And when he did get out he couldn't stand up straight. He was so weak and cold we had to get under each arm and help him to the cafe.

I sat down next to Jerry at a table and Levi sat across from us. We ordered coffee and after about half-a-dozen cups, Jerry began to thaw out. At least his lips weren't blue anymore.

"You know, Jerry," I said, "You not only missed a great party last night, but your girlfriend showed up looking for you."

"Damn you! I . . . I . . ."

"Oh hell, Jerry! Take what life gives you and make the most of it. She wasn't all that bad. Besides me and ole Levi here have done a lot worse."

Of course, that got us both started telling stories about just how bad some of our dates had been. We had a horror story for every occasion and we thought each one was funnier than the next. Jerry on the other hand, couldn't see any humor in it at all, but that was okay with us. Levi and me were laughing enough for all three of us.

When the folks next to me left their table I reached

over and got their leftover toast and jelly and sat it down between us.

"Help yourself, Jerry."

He looked embarrassed. I guess he was surprised thay anyone would do such a thing. The waitress looked at me and shook her head. She poured Jerry another cup of coffee.

"Why are you hanging out with this rowdy pair?" she asked him.

"It's not by choice, ma'am." He turned to me. "See! Even the waitress knows I don't belong here."

Levi reached over and grabbed another plate off the table next to us. He finished off the leftover scraps and washed them down with a mouthful of coffee.

"Do you have to do that?" Jerry muttered.

"A man ought never let good food go to waste," I said. "Are you sure you don't want some breakfast?"

About the time the waitress headed over to clean off the table she noticed something sticking out of Jerry's windbreaker.

"What's this, Honey?"

She yanked a pair of Levi's dirty shorts out from under his collar, then dropped them like they'd bit her — right beside Jerry's coffee cup. His face turned red as a stoplight. Levi bust out laughing and I picked up the shorts and hurled them across the table.

"Here. These are yours."

Levi tossed them back at me.

"No they're not," he hollered. "Yours are the ones with the yellow stripe. Remember?"

"No sir. I believe these here are Jerry's."

When I stuffed the shorts into Jerry's jacket pocket

34

his face turned white as a ghost — kind of translucent-like.

"That's it!" he screeched. "I'm getting out of here."

He tried to stand up, but I held him by the arm.

"Wait a minute, Jerry. We're just having a little fun. Besides, how are you going to get a ride out of here?"

"I'll find a way. I'll ask one of those truckers over there at the counter."

"You're gonna have to wear a skirt and shave your legs if you want to ride with a trucker."

"I'll pay someone to take me home. I don't care what I have to do. I'm getting out of here. Where's the phone in this place?"

Levi and me glanced around the cafe, pretending to look for a phone.

"Guess who?"

I don't know where she came from, but when I looked back in Jerry's direction, there was Laverne standing behind him with her hands over his eyes. Man, I just couldn't take it. I laughed so hard coffee shot out of my nose. I figured all that was left for Jerry to do now was go in the bathroom and hang himself.

Laverne uncovered Jerry's face and leaned over the table.

"Hi, Sugar. I saw the truck parked outside and I just stopped in to say good-bye."

"Good-bye?" Jerry squeaked.

"Yea, I gotta go home today so I can be back in time for work."

"Where do you live?" Jerry asked.

"Oh, a long way from here, Honey. Tucumcari."

Jerry's eyes brightened as she smoothed his hair across the top of his head. He'd forgotten all about how he might look. But Laverne didn't care. When he felt the top of his head and gave her a hopeless sort of grin, she just patted his shoulder and told him not to worry about it.

"I wish I could stay and watch the rest of the show with you, but I really have to go."

Jerry grabbed Laverne's arm like it was the rip cord on a parachute.

"How'd you like some company?"

I looked over at Levi. His eyebrows were arched clear up under the brim of his hat. I guess Laverne couldn't believe her ears, either.

"What? And miss the rest of the rodeo? You mean you'd rather ride home with me than your buddies?"

"Yea. I *really* want to go with you."

A smile as big as a brush fire spread across Laverne's face.

"I didn't think you were ever gonna give up playing hard to get. Cutie."

Jerry stood up and put his arm around Laverne's waist. I think it was the first time I'd seen him smile.

"I ain't easy," he said, "But I can be had."

THE HAT

Cowboys see a lot of funny things, but no one has done a better job of putting them on paper than western cartoonist, Ace Reid. Whoever said "a picture is worth a thousand words" must have been talking about Ace Reid. No other artist understood the predicaments cowboys get in better than ole Ace. He'd draw some poor cowboy in a wreck with an old cow or a broncy horse, then add a hilarious caption underneath — something only a cowboy would say. I especially liked his calendars. I bought a new one every year, even when I was on the road. I kept one in my car, too. I always wanted to write to Ace about some things that happened to me. I hoped he might be able to capture them on paper, too, so people could get a picture of how funny some of the stuff I've seen really was. Of course, I never got around to contacting ole Ace. But if I had, I think I would have told him about the time I went down the road with Buck. I was just a teenager, but I'll never forget it.

I rode in my first rodeo when I was fifteen years old. Me and some other kids saved up our money and entered together. We got our heads busted and my buddies retired from rodeo as soon as we got home. I, on the other hand, possessed those rare and admirable qualities that make up a true rodeo cowboy — I was totally nuts and too stupid to be scared. I was hooked from that first show, and just as soon as I could drive, I left home to pursue my career.

I probably would have made out okay on my own, but I owe a lot to some of the older guys I met in the early days. They all agreed I had one hell of a potential, even if I hadn't fully demonstrated it, yet. What I needed was one of those mentors — someone to teach me the finer points of riding saddle broncs. During five years of amateur shows and eleven years in RCA, I had me quite a few of them mentors, but old Buck was the first.

When I was about eighteen I heard about a rodeo school. I'd been wanting to put some polish on my riding style and a school sounded like a good place to do it. The other cowboys said the guy who ran this here school got really tanked up sometimes, but he sure enough knew about riding broncs. Buck was an old hand. He had covered many a bucking horse and he sounded just like the guy I was looking for. So, off I went to *Buck's School of Bronc Riding*.

The first time I saw ole Buck there was something out of place about him. He was wearing a pair of faded Wranglers and a striped shirt with two buttons missing and sleeves at least an inch too short. His boots were nearly worn smooth and he had the prettiest hat I ever saw. That was it — the hat! It was light gray-colored and looked brand new. Not a speck of dust.

He seemed like a nice enough guy, so I walked up and introduced myself.

"Hoss, Casey here will show you to the bunkhouse. Put your gear in there and come on out. We'll ride the hair off some of these broomtails."

"Yes, sir!"

"That sure is a nice hat ole Buck's wearing," I said to Casey as I followed him to the bunkhouse.

Casey laughed. "Yea. Ain't that the damnedest thing you ever seen? Ole Buck looks like he buys his clothes at the Salvation Army. He believes in getting his money's worth out of his duds, but he always wears the best hat money can buy, and drives the biggest car in town. Wait till you see his Lincoln."

I was at the school about a week and I got on forty head of saddle broncs, making a hand. Ole Buck just took a liking to me right off. I thought I was doing pretty good and I guess he did, too.

"Hoss," he said to me one day, "Why don't you get a permit and go on up to Oklahoma with me and make a rodeo. With a little luck and some help I think you might make a hand."

Let me tell you, my head got as big as a No. 2 washtub. Here I was being asked by a sure-enough hand to go down the road with him. I had been waiting for this all my life, and even though my insides were a-jumping, I wasn't going to let anything stand in my way. So, I said:

"Sure! Why not?"

By next morning I had my war bag packed and ready to go. I met Buck out in front of the arena.

"We'll take my rig, Hoss."

I was sure glad to hear that. My old pickup didn't run too good. I had to turn the steering wheel three times before it took hold, and pump the brakes hard and fast just to slow down — which worked okay, except for sudden stops. So, it was a big relief to me that Buck wanted to go in his car.

I climbed in on the passenger's side and Buck and his big ole hat got in behind the steering wheel of his brand-new '61 Lincoln. It had power steering and air conditioning. I couldn't remember if I'd ever been in a car with air conditioning before. It had power brakes, too. Yes sir! That sucker could stop on a dime. All you had to do was barely tap them. Already I was beginning to feel like a bigshot.

"I sure like your rig, Buck."

"Thank you, Hoss. I'm rather partial to it myself. The Lincoln is a gal-fetching machine, too."

"That right?"

"Oh, yea. I got me a new wife to go with every one I've had. This here's my fifth."

"Fifth car or fifth wife?"

"Both!"

"I don't think I want any wives just yet."

"Oh, don't worry about that none. You don't have to marry them, anyways. I'm just an old-fashioned kind of guy. I like to make an honest woman out of them. You know what I mean?"

I nodded, just to be agreeable. Buck sure knew a lot about life. I was sort of studying him — watching and listening as we drove down the road — but I couldn't take my eyes off his hat.

"That's about the best looking hat I ever seen."

"It's a dandy all right," he said, petting the brim like it was the neck of a fast Texas quarter horse.

"This here is a silver belly Stetson — prettiest hat ever made. And this is called the cattleman's crease."

"The cattleman's crease?"

"Yep! Most cowboys like to shape their own hats, you know. I've been wearing this crease for twenty-five years."

He took his hat off and handed it to me. I looked it over and turned it upside down. Inside, ten X's were

40

printed on the sweatband.

"What are the X's for?"

"Ten X beaver. That's what it means. The more X's on a Stetson the more beaver fur is in the hat. Beaver fur is the best hat-making material there is."

I decided right then and there I was going to have me a hat like that.

"I'm about due for a new hat," I said.

"A hat makes a cowboy, Hoss. But you got to learn the rules before you deserve to wear a bonnet like this. Best know how to make love before you get yourself a girl, if you know what I mean."

He turned and grinned at me. I handed him his hat and he pushed it back down on his head. Now, I figured I already knew plenty about women, but I wanted to know more about that hat.

"What are the rules, Buck?"

"First of all, it's bad manners to wear a hat indoors. And I don't care what those idiots in Dallas do, a real cowboy never wears his hat on the dance floor."

I already knew that, too, but I never had heard what Buck was fixing to tell me next.

"Never let another man wear your hat. When you have a good bonnet like this, all kinds of dudes come up and want to try it on. Touching a man's hat in an invitation to fight, pure and simple. But the most important thing is . . . *never* put your hat on the bed."

"Don't put it on the bed?"

"That's right. Bad luck. Worst luck you can possibly have. A cowboy needs more than just skill, he needs luck, too. And another thing . . . any wife who throws your hat on the bed is asking for a divorce."

41

I figured if anyone knew about wives and divorces, it ought to be old Buck.

"Did your wife ever throw your hat on the bed?"

"Yep. That's what happened to the last one. She no sooner tossed my hat on the bed than I tossed her right out the door. I won't tolerate rudeness in a woman."

I had already learned about hats, luck and women and we hadn't even got out of town. All of a sudden Buck peeled into a parking lot and sped up to a liquor store.

"Going to get us a pint. Get us oiled up a little bit. It sure makes this car ride better."

I didn't know how a car could ride any better than that Lincoln but it was a long trip to Oklahoma and sipping a bit while we were going down the road seemed to be a good idea. At least Buck thought so, and he had been right about everything so far. He got out of the car, cocked his hat to one side and strolled into the liquor store. A minute later he came out with a half-gallon jug.

"They had such a good deal on this hooch I just couldn't pass it up. This ought to get us as far as Ponca City."

I thought to myself, a jug like that would get me plum to California. But I didn't want to seem like a lightweight, so I kept my mouth shut.

Now, even though ole Buck had a big fancy car, he hated to drive. Like most cowboys that have been rodeoing any time at all, he was road foundered.

"I like to drink whiskey going to the rodeo," he said. "And sleep coming back."

That only meant one thing. I had just got promoted to chauffeur. That suited me just fine. Since I'd never driven a big car like this before, I was happy to oblige. We switched places and I settled into the soft leather seat behind the steering wheel, gripped it with both hands and took off like I knew what I was doing.

Buck pulled his hat down like he was coming out of the chute and proceeded to pour drinks for both of us. Now, I'd drank before, but mostly it was hooch from the local bootleggers, or some rotgut stuff me and my buddies went together to buy. This stuff was smooth. I mean it went down real easy . . . gave me a warm tingling feeling from my head to my toes. I thought I'd died and gone to heaven. Ole Buck sure had good taste. Cars, hats, whiskey, you name it. This was definitely the only way to travel to Oklahoma.

At that time, in Oklahoma, they had a toll road. We had to stop on the way in and get a ticket, then pay a toll when we got off. Buck was drinking about as fast as he was pouring, so he didn't see the toll booth until we were almost on top of it. He was trying to explain it all to me when he caught sight of it.

"Stop at the booth, Hoss," he hollered. "This is where we get our ticket."

I pulled up to the booth and that's when I knew those brakes were going to take some getting used to. I think we were both suffering a mild case of whiplash, but Buck kept pouring the drinks and soon we forgot all about it. He seemed impressed with me so far, and I wasn't about to let him think I couldn't keep up with him, so I matched him drink for drink.

It was one hundred and fifty miles between the toll booth and where we wanted to get off. Two men can drink a lot of whiskey in a hundred and fifty miles, especially with ole Buck pouring. He drank at least a fifth a day

43

— every day. No one would know except that his left eye would cross, and you could never tell just what in the heck he was looking at. When that eye started to wander, I knew he was really high, and by the time we reached our exit, my eyes were starting to cross, too. That's when I realized I hadn't exactly been driving in a straight line.

"Goddamn, Hoss. That toll booth is coming up real fast. I'd better get that ticket out of the glove box."

I wanted to get the car straight before we reached the booth so I cranked the wheel to the right a little. That power steering was sure touchy. When I seen we were headed for the shoulder I pulled back the other direction. Buck slammed up against the door just as he was about to unlatch the glove box. Due to our liquor consumption, neither one of us was navigating too good. He reached and grabbed my arm.

"Just hold her steady there, Hoss."

He sat straight up, gripped the dash with one hand to steady himself and took another swipe at the latch. Well, he got it open this time, but his vision was so blurred he had to put his head down real close to look inside for the ticket. When he couldn't see it right off, he began throwing old maps and crumpled scraps of paper all over the car.

"Here it is! No, damn it, that ain't it."

Another map went sailing into the back seat.

"Hold on, Hoss, I found it. Shit! That ain't it either."

Buck was sifting though that glove box like he was panning for gold, and I was starting to have difficulty keeping that Lincoln on the road. Between watching Buck and trying to focus on the hood of the car — everything past that was all fuzzy — I damned near didn't see the toll booth until it was right in front of us. Without thinking about those power brakes, I rared back and hit the pedal as hard as I could. Next thing I knew we were doing donuts all over that highway. When we finally stopped, the impact drove old Buck's head right into that glove box, hat and all.

Incredible as it may seem, we landed smack-dab in front of the booth. The guy inside was froze stiff and his mouth was stuck open like he had lockjaw. It wasn't bad enough that two drunk cowboys had nearly crashed into his toll booth, but when I rolled the window down, the smell about knocked him cold. A considerable amount of whiskey had spilled and we were half-soaked. Buck had managed to get his head out of the glove box and what a sight he was! I don't believe I ever saw anything in my life as funny as him with that hat jammed down on his head. The crown was clear over his ears and the brim was tore half off, hanging around his neck like a bib. He peeked through the tiny slit between the two halves of his prize Stetson and it was then I realized that both his eyes were crossed.

"Here it is. I found the ticket, Hoss."

"Don't we need some money?" I asked.

Buck had a hell of a time getting his hand in his pocket. He was do dizzy that when he finally found some change, he gave me all he had. There must have been at least three bucks worth of quarters and half-dollars, but I didn't know how much the toll was, so I turned it all over to the guy in the booth. He never said a word, just kept staring at us as he reached for the money, his hand just a-quivering. He managed a half-hearted smile that looked more like a nervous twitch, and as soon as he had the money in his hand, he slammed the window shut. And I swear I saw him lock it.

"Keep the change!" Buck hollered as we spun out down the highway.

"Eeeee Haaaa!" I yelled and let the hammer down.

Buck was still trying to see up from under the crown of his Stetson — or out and over the brim. I wasn't sure which. Finally, he grabbed the brim with both hands and tugged hard until he got it pried off his head, and then he looked at me with them crossed eyes and said:

"Hoss, you sure are hard on them brakes."

He looked down at what was left of his bonnet.

"And damn hard on hats, too!"

Yes, sir. Now, wouldn't that have made a dandy picture for the month of July?

BRUSH POPPIN

When I was younger and even more foolish, I cowboyed on ranches to make a few bucks between shows. Being a professional rodeo cowboy in the old days was not nearly so profitable as it is now. We had to find ways to get by when we hit a bad streak.

It was on a northern New Mexico ranch where I met Orville, a team roper. Orville was the runt of the litter — short, so skinny he had to run around in the shower to get wet, and bowlegged, to boot! He looked like he'd been born with a rain barrel between his legs. Always had a silly-looking grin on his face, too, even when there was absolutely nothing to grin about. His top lip curled up just enough to expose his long gums and stubby teeth. I have to admit, being around Orville kept things interesting. He was full of surprises, mainly because he was just too dull to think of the consequences of a situation before it presented itself.

So, there we both were on the high plains and winter coming on fast. We had just finished working some cattle that were going on wheat pasture. The wind and dust was blowing hard, like it always does when you work cattle. Orville had his collar pulled up and was sunk down in his jacket so all you could see was his red-rimmed eyes staring out. But that didn't keep the dirt from whirling up around his horse and blowing in his face. I think it's the law. Every time you work cattle the wind blows up a storm, and it's either cold as the dickens or hot as Hades, but it's never nice. I was sitting on my horse shivering. I looked at Orville. He was doing the same.

"Orville, I'm sick of this wind and cold. There ain't but ten trees on these old plains and they're all growing at a forty-degree angle. It's no wonder all the people round here walk leaning into the wind. Then, on the one day of the year it don't blow, they fall down face first and can't walk at all. I sure don't want to spend another winter here. Let's go winter up some place where it's a little warmer and the wind don't blow the bark of the fence posts."

"Hoss, that sounds like a good idee to me. Let's load up Ole Blue and set out first thing in the morning."

So that's just what we did. I started packing all my worldly possessions: a pair of Wranglers, two shirts, a couple of ropes, a worn-out saddle blanket, a curry comb, a deck of cards, an Ace Reid calender, and an old issue of *Western Horseman*. Orville stuffed his four shirts, all of them blue, into his war bag.

"Say, Orville, just how in the world do you decide which shirt you're gonna wear every day?"

He looked into his bag, then at me, and back at the shirts again.

"I wear the clean one."

Orville liked to keep things simple.

Ole Blue was Orville's '57 DeSoto. The car was red when he got it, but he said it reminded him of a fire truck. It was about as big as one, too. Well, one day he found some blue paint a farmer had been using to paint his tractor. He borrowed a brush and gave that big tank a shiny new blue coat — bumper and all. That's how she got her name. Orville was partial to blue. Trouble is, a whirlwind came by about that time and plastered sand all over the wet paint.

Yes, sir, Ole Blue had to be the ugliest car in all

48

of New Mexico! She looked like a blue Appaloosa with brown spots. But we figured she'd get us there. Besides, we didn't really have much choice. I had wrecked my pickup the month before when this girl I was going with took out after me with a shotgun. I peeled out of her drive and was going about sixty when I turned around to see how close she was. That's when I ran into a big old round bale that had fallen off a flatbed and landed right in the middle of the road. But that's another story.

Ole Blue's back doors were wired shut so I shoved our saddles and war bags through the front window and threw them over the seat. Orville fired her up and I made sure the baling twine holding the hood down was good and tight before we took off.

"I know a couple of fellas down in Texas who might steer us to where we could cowboy up for the winter," Orville said after we'd bumped down the dirt road a mile or two.

"You know, I ain't been to Texas in awhile. Sounds pretty good to me. A dose of South Texas would probably cure what ails us."

So we left New Mexico and headed for Texas. I was having a hard time getting comfortable in Ole Blue. I was used to a pickup. There wasn't enough room for my long legs and I had to fold them up with my knees almost to my chin. The headliner, which was torn in several places, was resting on top of my head, and Orville had slid the seat up as far as he could to reach the brakes. The heater didn't work, either. The farther we went the colder it got. It must have been eighty below. The only blankets we had were our saddle blankets, which we wrapped around us Indian style. Judging from the strange

49

looks we got when we drove through them little podunk towns, I'll bet we were a sight.

You couldn't drive Blue. You had to just kind of herd her in the general direction you wanted her to go. Two of the tires were slick and the brakes were metal-to-metal. We'd have to pump them like hell before she'd slow down. It was a tricky operation if anything got in our way. But, cowboys are lucky, and we had no doubt we would get some place before long.

That some place turned out to be Mineral Wells.

"I got a friend that runs a riding stable on the army base here," Orville told me. "He's an old cowboy and he knows all the ranchers in this part of the country. If anybody would know where we could find a job, it'd be Pappy."

"Well, that sounds like the best plan we got. I've always been partial to Mineral Wells anyway."

Fort Walters was a big base — about ten thousand acres — but at that time it was only being used to train helicopter pilots. And there weren't a whole lot of them. Pappy's place was on the base.

It was near dark when we pulled up in front of the riding stables where Pappy was feeding the horses. As we were walking toward the stables Orville turned to me and half whispered:

"Uh, I'm not too sure how Pappy is going to receive us."

"What are you talking about?"

"I used to go with his daughter, but she was getting a little too serious for me so I pulled up one night and left."

"And . . . ?"

"Well, I sort of neglected to tell her I was leaving."

"Oh, that's just great, Orville! When were you planning to let me in on this little secret — before or after we start picking buckshot out of our butts?"

"Don't go getting your feathers up. I'm telling you now. I don't think it's gonna be a big problem. It's been two years, and I'm sure she and her daddy have both forgotten all about it by now."

I guessed Orville thought because his memory was poor, everyone else's was too.

"I hope to hell you're right, because if you're not, me and her daddy will have a fight to see which one of us is going to kill you first!"

Now there's two things that make me real snakey — any old momma cow on the prod and a girl's daddy on the prod. I went to sort of shuffling my feet and looking for a place to run and that's when old Pappy turned around, seen Orville, and let out a blood-curdling yell. It scared me half to death because I still wasn't sure I liked the way Orville was finding out if the water was clear. I positioned myself near the door in case I needed to make a quick getaway, and kept watching Pappy for any sudden movements. He had plenty of weapons around — a hay hook on the wall, a pitchfork leaning against the stall door, and there was no telling whether or not he was packing a gun. Texans are notorious for exercising their second-amendment rights.

I was surprised when Pappy grabbed Orville and went to pounding him on the back, saying how glad he was to see him, and all that other B.S. At first I thought it might be a trap, because Orville had a history of leaving out little details that could get you killed. But after a bit I figured no blood was going to be spilled so I relaxed.

"Pappy, this is my partner, Dan. Everyone just calls

51

him Hoss. We're both looking for some cowboy work. You know anybody that needs a couple of good hands?"

Pappy looked up at me and shook my hand.

"How you all doing?" he said real friendly like. "You boys couldn't have timed it any better. Come on in the office. We'll have a cup of coffee."

His office was an eight-by-ten tack room with three bales of hay stacked in the corner and two old lawn chairs with frayed nylon webbing and twisted aluminum frames. On top of a washtub turned upside down was a coffee pot, a jelly jar full of sugar, six or seven paper cups — most of them used already — and a Del Monte green beans can Pappy used for a spit cup. A horse in the next stall over had kicked plum through the wall, and an Ace Reid calendar half-covered the hole. A lightbulb hanging in the center of the room had a churchkey attached to its cord so Pappy could find it in the dark — or open a cold Coors.

I watched Orville as he eased into one of the lawn chairs. It give a little so I decided to play it safe and settled on a bale a hay. I wasn't real heavy back then, but pretty big for a bullrider. At six-four and two hundred pounds I had been known to fold a few aluminum chairs in the past.

Pappy looked to be about fifty-five. His black wavy hair was parted down the side so a patch of it hung over his left eye. He wasn't all that tall, but he made up for it in width. He had a big barrel chest and a beer-belly roll that nearly covered his belt. When he poured us some coffee and I took a sip, I knew right then and there how he was going to get even with Orville — make us drink that coffee! You could have used it for road patch.

I scrunched my face up, held my breath and swallowed hard. I probably should've chewed it first. Believe it or not, Orville was enjoying his. But then he'd drink horse piss if it had a head on it. I added a couple of spoonfuls of sugar to mine, stayed quiet, and just listened to the two of them jawing. After awhile Pappy reached in his pocket for his Redman pouch, stuffed a wad in his cheek and sat down on the other lawn chair.

"Lucky you fellas showed up when you did. Just last week the commander came down to ask me if I knew of any cowboys who could catch the wild cattle that's been running on the base."

According to Pappy, the Army boys didn't know nothing about nothing. One night about midnight, two young MP's — city boys from back east — were out on patrol when they came across a big Brahma bull standing in the road. They never had seen a cow before, let alone a Brahma bull. They laid on the horn, thinking that would make him move.

Pappy spit in the bean can and continued.

"That ole bull took exception to them boys trying to make him move. He was a big sucker! And he wasn't all that fond of horns blowing in his face, either. He charged the jeep. Stuck a horn plum through the radiator, broke out the headlights, and blowed snot all over it. Then, after those Yankee boys jumped out and took off a-hooking it for headquarters, he pretty well went on to tear the rest of it apart, too."

Orville and I were both in stitches.

"I sure wish I could have seen that," Orville said to Pappy.

"Oh, I wish I could have, too. I guess they were scared out of their wits. They was screaming they'd been attacked by a wild animal and the whole base was put on a

53

special alert. They even sent armed patrols out to kill that marauding beast. Now, ain't that the damnedest thing you ever heard?"

Pappy hee-hawed and slapped his knee.

"Did they find the bull?" I asked.

"Hell no! The worst part is, they called and woke up the commander in the middle of the night to tell him a crazed animal was running all over the base. He'd been raised on a farm and had a pretty good idea what had happened, though. He got them two MP's calmed down real quick."

Pappy stood up and headed in my direction with the coffee pot. I put my hand over the top of my cup.

"No thanks. I'm still sipping on this first one. So what did the commander have to say?"

"The next day he was a little red-eyed from losing sleep, but he got over it. Said if I knew of some cowboys that could get those critters out he would let them have the cattle for nothing, just to get rid of them. If not, he was going to have to shoot them, 'cause he couldn't have them tearing up government property and scaring the hell out of his troops."

Orville seemed to think that was pretty damned funny and the two of us started laughing again.

"Sounds like those old boys scare pretty easy," I said. "It would be a shame to shoot that bull."

"Well, I told him I'd try and find somebody to get him out of here. Them cattle is worth some money. I didn't tell him how much money, because it could be a pretty good chunk and the Army might want some of it. Then you boys showed up. How's that for luck?"

"Well, Hoss," Orville smiled as he got out of his

chair. "Maybe we made a good draw at this place after all."

I was still a little suspicious but I didn't say anything.

"You know, a couple of good cowboys like you two should be able to get those cattle out of there in no time at all."

I guessed Pappy was a lot like Orville when it came to details. He forgot to mention we were the only two stupid enough to try. We found out later that he had called some other boys to do the job, but they had just laughed at him. Told him there wasn't a cowboy in all of Texas dumb enough to go out after them cattle. Of course, they didn't know me and Orville had showed up.

Pappy said he would furnish the horses and let us stay at the stables for twenty-five percent of the sales. Being's how we had nothing to lose but time, it seemed like a good deal. It was the best offer we'd had in a long time. Hell, it was the only offer we'd had! Besides, we were too tired to argue. Pappy found a couple of old sleeping bags stowed behind the hay bales, and we rolled them out right there on his office floor. I barely remember saying good-night.

When I woke up the next morning I stepped outside to survey the country. There was a lot of it. During World War II, Fort Walters was used for training infantry. But the Army had let the biggest part of the base grow up in brush since then, and it had gotten real thick. Except for a clearing around the airstrip where the helicopters were, all you could see was brush. And there was no telling how many head of cattle was in there.

After years of neglect, most of the fences were gone and cattle from neighboring ranches had wandered onto the base. Now, cattle get used to cowboys feeding them from the back of a truck, and they usually come a-running every time they hear a horn honk. But nobody was feeding the ones at Fort Walters. Because it was government property, the ranchers weren't allowed to round up their strays, and after awhile the whole herd turned wild as weeds.

Where I was raised, on the New Mexico-Texas border, there's hardly any brush to speak of. This stuff reminded me of an overgrown prickly nest. I had never seen anything like it. Live oak, scrub oak and blackjack oak was thick as hair on a dog. There was also mesquite, chaparral and some other brush I'd never seen before. I had cowboyed in the mountains in New Mexico, the Texas panhandle and Arizona, too, but there wasn't anything resembling this mess. Every bit of it had thorns. I had no idea what I was getting myself into and, boy, was I in for an education.

As I walked back inside to wake Orville up, I saw Pappy headed towards the stable with his green bean can in his hand.

"Morning boys. You ready to take a look at the horses yet?"

After Orville put on a clean blue shirt we went to take a gander at the horses. When Orville picked the two smallest ones, I figured the reason he wanted the runts of the litter was because he was so small himself. As for me, if I had a choice, I always rode a pretty fair-sized horse — one that I wasn't afraid to tie on to anything. But I didn't know, before this little adventure was over with, I'd be looking for a Shetland.

We saddled up and rode out to get a feel for the place and see if we could spot any tracks or find where the cattle watered at. As we rode I got an up-close look at what we would be chasing those animals through, and I began to have doubts about the wisdom of this expedition. There were little clearings here and there, and trails that turned back on theirself, then ran right back into the brush. It was so thick you couldn't see ten yards in front of you. Everything in there had four-inch thorns on it, and them cow trails ran right into it. I felt my blood start to run cold. It was about then I went to asking questions.

"Orville, have you ever done this kind of cowboying before?"

He just looked at me with that silly grin of his and said: "Could be."

"How in the world do you get cattle out of country like this?"

"You just pull your hat down real low, hold on tight and ride like hell."

"Well, this is a fine time to turn into some kind of philosopher. All I want to do is stay warm until winter is over and get a little money in my pocket before the next rodeo season. I don't want to have my skin sanded off in this jungle brush. I just want to do a job and get on down the road.

"That's exactly what we're gonna do, Hoss."

I didn't believe him, but our options were somewhat limited at the time. We rode the biggest part of the day, checking out the lay of the land and trying to spot some cattle. We could hear them, but I only caught a glimpse of one cow. There's a reason boots and saddles are made from cowhide — it's tough. Those cows could shoot between those thorns without it slowing them down the least little bit. When they broke a hole through a wall of trees and brush, the dead wood snapped off and went flying in every direction. Sounded like a train running through an empty barn.

The cattle were a mix of every breed you could think of. Some were Brahma and Angus, others were Hereford and Longhorn. And according to the MP's, the bull they had encountered was a cross between a buffalo and a mountain lion. Whatever he was, I figured our chances of finding him in that brush were about nil.

I had never worked in this part of Texas before, and I didn't know nothing about brush poppin, so when we got back to the the stables I had a few questions for Pappy. I swear he looked half surprised that we even found our way back.

"Pappy, those cattle sure are spooked. Why is that?"

Pappy looked down and spit, barely missing the toe of my boot.

"Probably on account of the pilots. They get a real charge outta making a pass at them with the helicopters — when they find a few head out in the open, that is. Sometimes they might make a run at them with the jeep, too. Not that big ole bull, though. He'll chase you in a heartbeat. They stay away from him."

"Great!" I looked hard at Orville. "I can get closer to the deer than the cattle. And there's a big ole hooking bull just hiding out there in the weeds waiting to eat my lunch. Got anymore good news?"

Orville cocked his hat back, like he always did when he was fixing to get sarcastic.

"Nope. You're just going to have to cowboy up and make a hand if you're going to get them out. That's how the old cowboys did it."

"Yea! And those old cowboys died at a real early age, too. I suppose you didn't think about that. Did you?"

Pappy seemed to be enjoying our differences of opinion. Orville stepped down off his little pony and Pappy just kept spitting, chewing and chuckling as we continued to insult each other.

"See, Pappy. Hoss here is more of a lover than a fighter. He'd rather pick up a cute little filly and tell her one of his wild west stories than rustle cattle. Fact is, some of them women give him more misery than a bunch of ornery cattle. That's why we had to drive Ole Blue . . ."

I interrupted him: "You don't seem to mind when one of those women has a friend that's just dying to meet a cowboy, too."

Pappy finally lost interest.

"When you kids are done fighting, let me know. There's a lot of work to do tomorrow."

I didn't want to admit it right then and there, but Orville was right. My ideal life was riding bulls and saddle broncs . . . and rubbing belt buckles with a rodeo queen or two . . . and I was eager to get back to it.

Next morning we started early. A mile or so away from the stables we came across ten head of cows and yearlings. They had found an opening — about three-acres, but no more. We took off after them. My horse could really move, but so could those cows. I had just swung my rope once when he hit the brush. Timber was flying and I was a-ducking limbs, laying on one side of the saddle and then the other. That ole pony never weakened, but I had forgot to tuck my loop in. That damn rope forked a limb and sucked me off that horse like a new Hoover. I landed flat on my back.

Talk about letting the air out of a man. It must have been five minutes before those stupid birds stopped chirping. It was my own fault. I never was a great roper, so I always swung a big loop. They used to say I could rope two cows at once, but from then on that loop would barely fit over a turtle's neck. I got up and staggered over to where my horse was grazing, stepped on, and away we went. I took after a couple more cows but never even got close. After easing through that jungle for four hours, I finally ran across Orville.

"Hey, Orville. How are you faring? I haven't caught a thing."

He took one look at me and laughed till I thought he'd fall off his horse. I didn't see that it was all that funny, but then Orville always did have a sick sense of humor. When he finally got to where he could talk, he said:

"I thought we were trying to rope cattle. You look like you been wrestling a grizzly bear."

I guess I did look the worse for wear. My hands were scratched up real bad and sticks were poking out every which way. I felt like a hungover porcupine. The crease in my hat had been changed about ten times, which wouldn't have been so bad but my head was in it at the time. I had so many knots on my head I knew it would be real painful if I tried to pull my hat off, so I just left it pushed down over my ears. Every time Orville looked at me he would bust out laughing again.

"Look, you little runt, I wouldn't get near so beat up if I could hide behind the saddle horn like you."

Orville had managed to collect a few thorns himself, so when I suggested we head back to the stables and change horses, he was raring to go. Pappy was right there waiting to hear the news.

"I didn't know you boys were in the land-clearing business," he snickered.

That's all I needed. One more smart aleck. We unsaddled our horses, pulled the thorns out of them and started treating their cuts and bruises with some foul-smelling concoction Pappy had made up.

"What the hell is in this stuff?" I asked.

"Aw, just a little coal oil, turpentine . . . No, I think it was chili peppers and . . . Wait a minute!" He scratched his behind a minute, then let fly a yard of spit. "It's liniment, damn it! Bacon grease, tobacky juice. Oh hell, you know . . . the usual."

After we got the horses taken care of, we started working on ourselves. Orville complained that his hands were scratched up so bad they were numb. And I had so many holes in me, I was sure I wouldn't be able to hold water for a week.

"You boys better put a little of that horse treatment on yourselves. It'll keep you from getting infected."

Orville poured some into the palm of his hand and proceeded to rub it on his face and arms. Then he let out a squall like someone had stuck a branding iron to him. He started running. Boy, did he run! I thought I'd have to put some of that stuff on me just so I could catch him. But he doubled back and jumped in the horse tank. It was the most horrible racket you ever heard. That's when he got to discussing Pappy's ancestral heritage.

I kind of meandered over to the tank.

"Orville, do you always raise such a commotion when you take a bath?"

At that point he turned on me. While he was call-

61

ing us every name in the book, Pappy and me was trying to figure a way to put poor Orville out of his misery.

"You got any of that coffee left, Pappy?"

"Sure! Just what you need to perk you up."

"I ain't gonna drink it," I said. "I was going to use it for a bandage."

Pappy took offense at me making fun of his coffee, but he got over it real quick. I think he figured me and Orville would pack up and leave if we got real mad, and there wasn't no sense in making things worse than they already were.

Orville got out of the tank and shook like a bird dog coming out of a river, spraying me and Pappy both. I didn't think a human being his size could get that wet.

"You know, Orville" I said, "We're going to have to change our strategy if we hope to do more than just get beat up."

After he dried out a little, we went back to see if there was some other way to get those cows out of that brush. We found about three clearings where the cattle had hid the last time we were chasing them. They would hit a clearing, find an opening in the brush and take off in a different direction. So, I figured if one of us eased into the clearing and the other chased the cattle towards it, we might have a shot at dropping a rope on one of them.

"Okay, Hoss, but I'll do the roping. You knock down more timber and make a lot more noise than me."

He was right. So that was our strategy for the second day. We headed back to the stables.

When I woke up the next morning I got up ree-eal slow and wandered down to the corral. I don't think there was a spot on me that wasn't sore. And I wasn't the only one lame. That old horse I had been riding looked like he'd been run over by a truck. He was favoring one knee which was swelled up real good, so I picked out another horse — one that wasn't so tall.

With our new plan figured out, Orville eased on out to one of the clearings while I circled around to try and push some of the cattle to him. I found a few cows about the same place we had first seen them the day before. One look at me and they started running. I had hoped they wouldn't take off, but they lit out like a bear was after them. I had to fall in behind to make sure thay didn't cut back. That brush hadn't thinned out any, either. But I was prepared for it this time. I had stuffed a flour sack in the crown of my hat and wadded up some burlap sacks and tied them around my knees under my chaps. I had on a blanket-lined Levi coat and some stiff leather gloves I had borrowed from Pappy.

This horse wasn't as fast as the other one and he didn't have as much heart — or maybe he was just smarter. I really had to work on him to make him keep up, and that made him mad. Even with all that extra padding I still got the bark knocked off me because he kept running under limbs trying to knock me off.

We had just started down a steep knoll when a big old cow in front of us hit the bottom of it and put on her brakes. My horse couldn't stop in time and we ran over the top of her. Down we all went — horse, cow and cowboy in one big heap. That dang horse! In struggling to get up, he kicked me three times, then stood on my foot and pinned me to the ground. That cow had blood in her eyes. She straightened up and came after us just a-snorting and slinging snot in all directions. She stirred up so much dirt it looked like a cyclone was chasing her. There was no doubt in my mind that she was intent on putting some hurt on something — anything — and it looked like I was it. I don't know if she just couldn't see for the dust or she was mad at my horse for knocking her down, but she ran over me to get to him. When she hit him, he fell halfway over and my foot came unpinned. I must have forgot all about my injuries from the day before, because when I saw that live oak nearby, I shot up it like a squirrel.

Now, all this had taken place in about half a minute, but it seemed like an eternity. I tried to holler for Orville but I didn't have any air again. I thought, they sure need to get some oxygen in this country, and that's when I saw that old cow come back. Was she mad! My horse had escaped, and with nothing else to terrorize, she seemed content to rearrange the dirt around the tree and perform a Mexican hat dance on my hat, which she had found a long ways from my head, thank God! I latched on to that tree tighter than its bark. You couldn't have blown me loose with dynamite.

Fear is a wonderful thing. It can make you do things you wouldn't be capable of doing otherwise.

After what seemed like an hour, I got my wind back enough to yell for Orville. I hoped he was close enough to hear me. The cow was still camped out under my tree. She had calmed down considerably, but I had a strong feeling I wouldn't be able to hang onto that tree as long as she could stand beneath it. She glared up at me and I stared down at my hat. A cowboy without a hat is like a gun without a trigger. I sure hated to lose my bonnet. Then I heard Orville.

"Where are you, Hoss?"

"Be careful!" I yelled. "There's an old cow over here and she sure enough has a bad attitude."

Orville started slapping his chaps and beating the brush with his hat as he came towards me. It worked. The old cow took one last look at me, then stuck her tail up and ambled off into the brush.

"Hoss, you look like a big old chicken sitting up there. Are you going to roost all day or are we going after some more cattle? I got one caught and tied up in the clearing already."

He stepped down and picked up my hat — or what was left of it — and near laughed himself silly.

"That cow really took a disliking to your sombrero. Maybe you should get another color. We don't want to stir these cattle up anymore than we have to."

I told him what he could do with his idea — and the hat.

"You know, Hoss, I don't think climbing trees agrees with you much. I had better go see if I can find your horse. I sure don't want to see you stumbling around out here getting yourself hurt."

I sat down and went to feeling around to see how much damage had been done. I had a gash on the side of my head and another on my ear where that dang horse had kicked my hat off, a swollen ankle where he stood on it, one eye starting to swell, and that cow had torn one sleeve half off my coat. I looked like I'd been attacked by a pitchfork. And with all those thorns sticking out of me, I felt like a big old pin cushion. I figured at this rate I'd be dead in two, maybe three, days.

When Orville got back with my horse, I pulled myself together and fixed my old hat as best I could. We rode up to the clearing where he had tied up his cow. She was still there. While Orville sat there admiring his handiwork I decided to ride over a ways and check out some trails. Building a loop as I rode, I was headed back into the brush when a two-year-old bull popped out right in front of me. I swung once and dropped my loop right around the little bull's neck. Little, hell! He probably weighed a thousand pounds, and that little horse of mine wasn't any more than eight hundred and fifty. I was going to have to work this just right or that bull would jerk him down in a minute and roll him up in a ball again just like that cow did.

The bull took off, and me right with him. I had my dally and was just fixing to turn off when we ran into Orville. He didn't see us in time to get out of the way, and my rope went up under the tail of his horse and he went to bucking. With my horse and that bull pulling in two different directions, the rope just kept shoving them closer to the trees. Orville had lost both stirrups and was about to get bucked off when the top of his head hit a big old limb, driving him clear back in the saddle. Meanwhile, I was a little busy myself, but every once in a while I caught a glimpse of my buddy. It seemed everytime he was about to get throwed off one side or the other, another tree would break his fall. One time I looked and he was sitting up around his horse's ears.

After I got that bull tied off to a tree I went looking for my partner. I sure hoped he hadn't been killed. He had all our money on him. I found him sitting on the ground holding his horse. He was beat to a pulp.

"Damn!" Orville winced. "I have never wanted to get bucked off so bad in my life, and I couldn't even fall off. I got shoved clear up that ole horse's neck and he threw his head up and loosened three of my teeth."

I was real sympathetic.

"Uh, Orville. You know, you are going to ruin that horse if you keep blindfolding him with your butt like that. Look at his mane. It's pulled out plum to his ears. How are we ever going to get these cattle out if you keep ruining all these perfectly good horses?"

Orville never did think much of my sense of humor. But then he'd got in a few digs on me earlier, and he knew that paybacks were hell.

We got those two back to the stables and put them in the round pen that Pappy used for breaking horses. It was stout, tall and not too big so they couldn't get a run and jump over the fence.

"I don't know about you," Orville said as he closed the gate, "But I could use some painkiller."

After knocking the biggest chunks of dirt off us, we got in Ole Blue and headed straight for a saloon. Now, Orville was sure thirsty, and he was going a might too fast for having bad brakes, but nothing I said would slow him down. We hit that parking lot just a-slinging gravel every which way. I warned him he better hit something cheap, so he ran into the dumpster, which had a whole bunch of empty bottles and cans stacked around it. That caused one helluva racket, but we got stopped. There was broken glass and beer cans all over the place. I was glad we hadn't hit anything too important, such as the shiny new pickup parked next to the building.

"Orville, you sure know how to make an entrance. Glad we ain't trying to sneak up on somebody."

"I was just trying to get here quick. I'm thirsty!"

People came running out of that saloon like it was

on fire, and the owner was jumping up and down, having a conniption fit. When he started screaming insulting remarks about crazy cowboys and such, we came crawling out of Ole Blue ready to fight. But he took one look at us and calmed right down. We must have looked like we were fighting bears all day with our battle scars and war-torn clothes and all. And I'm sure he could tell we weren't in the best of humor.

"Come on in, boys," he said with a forced smile. "The first drink is on the house."

That was definitely the best offer we'd had all day. We might near ran over him getting in the door. We'd both forgot our busted lips and loose teeth. Talk about making faces and doing a dance. That first one brought tears to our eyes. But we knew it would get better as the night wore on.

Some of the fellas in there were from the base. They asked if we were the two guys trying to catch those ferocious animals, and as soon as they opened their mouths we knew they were Yankees.

"Try hell!" I said. "We done caught a dozen or so, and we'll probably have the rest in a day or two."

Now a cowboy likes nothing better than to get some dudes together and tell wild west stories — especially this cowboy. Beat up as we were, I figured this bunch would believe just about anything we told them, so I started pouring it on thick. Orville helped, too. They ganged up around us with their mouths open as we told them about our daring-do's. Now, all this talking can make a man terrible thirsty, but they kept our throats well oiled. They were really lapping it up.

It turned out that one of those boys had been driving the jeep that got tore up by the old bull back at the base. After we listened to his side of the story, I offered him a few words of sympathy and a whole bunch of cowboy wisdom.

"Now, if you ever run into another bull, all you gotta do is hit him hard as you can right where the hair swirls in the center of his head. That's a real soft spot, just like on a baby's head. I guarantee you'll knock him out cold."

He was hanging on my every word.

"Gee," he slurred. "I appreciate the advice. I'll do that if I ever see one of those sons-of-bitches again."

He emptied his bottle of Coors, slammed it down on the table and ordered another round.

Overcome by his generosity, I proceeded to draw a little picture on a napkin to show him exactly where he ought to hit that bull the next time. Orville was still helping me out.

"Here!" he said, holding up his hand. "Pretend this is the swirl on that bull's noggin. Give it your best shot."

The kid hit his hand a couple of times, then me, not wanting to miss a golden opportunity . . . well, I just had to show him how it was done.

"You gotta hit him real hard. Like this."

I hit Orville's hand and knocked him right off his bar stool.

"See there," I grinned. "It works if you just hit the right spot hard enough."

Orville was mad, but he wasn't about to let those fellas know it.

"I think you boys got the hang of it," he muttered as he unfolded himself and climbed back on the stool.

The owner was biting his lip hard, trying not to laugh. After awhile he pulled me aside. Tears were streaming down his face.

"I ought to hire you two just to keep things lively around here. I'd give a month's wages to see that kid try that out on a bull."

I think we left shortly after that. I don't rightly remember. The next morning when we woke up in the stable, I figured we better check on Ole Blue and see if that dumpster had caused any serious damage. Also, we wanted to make sure there were no bodies under her. Considering all the free medicine we had consumed, her injuries were mild — a couple of whiskey bumps and one headlight hanging out of its socket. Nothing a piece of baling wire couldn't fix.

After applying a little first-aid, it was time to get back to work. We got to the clearings a half-hour after sunup and the cattle were already gone. That was a bad sign. We had hoped to have a few days before they wised up and went to hiding in the brush, but that's just the way it goes sometimes. Orville rode on to the clearing while I made a circle looking for fresh tracks. I found a spot where about a half-dozen or so had hit the brush. I eased onto their trail because I hadn't been on this one before. I wanted to see where it went. It didn't lead back to the clearing where Orville was, and I spotted two other trails and tracks leading to another clearing off in the other direction. These cattle had wised up real fast. They had moved out of the area where we were working them the day before, and if we were going to catch them, we were going to have to move, too. I rode back to tell my partner.

"Orville, those cattle are smarter than you, which

isn't all that impressive since everything I know is smarter than you. But we're going to have to move our little operation somewheres else because they are spooked of this part of the country."

Orville was too hungover to argue. We set out for those fresh tracks, but by noon we hadn't seen one cow. When we came across a deep gully with some tracks leading down into it, Orville was ready to take off hell-bent-for-election. But I wasn't in that big of a hurry.

"Let's think on this a bit," I said. "I don't want to be a-bustin brush if we don't have to. I think we otta sneak up on 'em. We could probably get a rope on them before they get to the brush, and those walls are too steep for them to climb."

"Okay, Hoss. But let's stick together this time. I don't want to have to be looking in every tree on this place to find you if you get knocked off your horse again."

"Very funny! Keep it up, comedian, and I'll run my rope up your nag's tail again."

"Well, are you ready? We gotta go in there sometime, Hoss."

"Lead the way, Daniel Boone."

We went down the gully real quiet so they wouldn't hear us and start to running. When we came around a bend, about halfway down, there was the biggest damn bull I had ever seen — and the meanest looking, too. His daddy must have been a Brahma and, from the size of his horns, his mammy must have been a moose. Mostly red-brindled with black stripes here and there, his neck was as big around as a barrel, and his tail was missing. He had plenty of battle scars, too. His big old floppy ears were split plum to his head and he had cold black eyes like a shark.

His horns weren't just for looks, either. He had used them. The ends weren't pointed anymore. They were worn off and frayed like he'd done battle with a Sherman tank. I knew he had to be the one that tore up the Army's jeep.

Soon as he saw us, he was on his feet. He didn't just get up . . . one second he was laying down and the next he was standing. I didn't know how anything that big could move that quick. There wasn't an ounce of fat anywhere on that massive body, just rippling muscle. I swear he must have been six foot at the hump and as long as a box car. A good ton for sure. Two thousand pounds of mean!

He faced us and shook his head. God, the set of racks he had! I was paying real close attention to everything he did, and so was my horse, which shows he was smarter than Orville who was sitting there shaking out a loop and acting like he was about to rope a milk calf.

Lucky for us, the bull ignored the rope and focused instead on a big tree trunk on the ground in front of him. He stuck a horn under it and flipped it twenty feet in the air like it was a twig. I swallowed hard. I knew this old boy wouldn't back down from anything, living or dead. I had seen what he could do to a jeep, and I had no hankering to see what he could do to a horse and a cowboy. I rode over and grabbed Orville's arm.

"Wait a damn minute! Think about this, Orville. That old boy will have us for supper."

Orville had that far-away look in his eye.

"Aw, Hoss. Nothing to sweat. He's just a big redneck. He looks like a big ole bubba to me. I never seen a bubba yet I couldn't whip. All blow and no go."

"Orville," I said real serious like with my chin on my

chest, "The only thing you can lick is your lips. If you stumble in there and drop a loop on Bubba in this gully, he'll turn us every which way but loose."

Never one to over-react when threatened with sure and sudden death, Orville became very indignant.

"We got him where we want him, Hoss. He can't climb out!"

"Neither can we," I had to point out. "And we don't have enough horse under us to handle something that big."

Orville thought just a second, which was about as long as he could hold any thought.

"I'll catch the horns. You pick up the heels."

Bubba started tearing up the ground around him and the horses, which were watching him with a whole lot of interest, started doing their let's-get-the-hell-out-of-Dodge dance. That bull had about heard all the arguing he needed to hear. He let out a bellow and charged. Our horses were gone! I don't mean they turned and run, they flat flew. Dang near snapped my head off, and throwing so much dirt in Bubba's face it's a wonder he didn't choke to death. And it's too bad he didn't.

Our horses were sure scared. We couldn't have begun to pull them up. No one had bothered to ask them what they thought about roping that freight train, so they had voted to leave, and leave in a hurry. They ran until they were plum out of that gully. We finally got them stopped, but they kept staring backwards, nervous as ticks. Orville looked a little nervous himself.

"Brother, that is one mean-ass bull!" he said to me like I might not have noticed.

"Orville, you have come up with some pretty hair-brained ideas in your life, but trying to rope that hooking son-of-bitch in a narrow gully was not one of your smartest. How was I supposed to get around behind him and pick up his heels?"

Orville grinned.

"It seemed like a good idee at the time."

After I cooled down a bit I had an idea of my own.

"Hell, we don't have to run anymore of these cattle. We'll just take these two ponies to the race track and get rich, since both of them can outrun a bullet."

"Yea," Orville laughed. "We'll get a big picture of Bubba and play a record of him bellowing and we'll win every race."

The way those two ponies were still tumbling, they would probably have died in the starting gates if they heard that bull again. I surveyed the situation.

"Orville, we might as well go back. These chicken-hearted horses won't be worth spit the rest of the day."

Back at the stables, Pappy was puttering around and mumbling to himself like he always did. When he seen us he knew something had happened because those two horses were still wild-eyed and jumpy. A bird flew over and my pony jumped sideways about ten feet, snorted, then swirled around and looked back the way we had come. We told Pappy what had happened. Of course, mine and Orville's stories weren't exactly identical. Pappy thought it was pretty funny, but he just could not understand why we hadn't roped that bull.

"Pappy," I said, "You're as nuts as Orville. If he had gotten a rope on him in that gully, there would have been pieces of horse and cowboys scattered all over this base. That old bull don't take prisoners."

Pappy changed the subject.

"Since you boys are back so early, we might as well load the cattle we got and take them to the sale barn."

We hooked up the stock trailer, fixed a chute to the round pen and backed the trailer up so we could get the gate closed easy. As soon as we opened it, that little bull I had caught took off down the alley like a shot with Orville's cow right behind him. They were charging full bore when they hit that trailer, and that dumb bull hit the front end so hard that the window popped out. He also left a big dent in the front of the trailer, which didn't please Pappy none and made the bull real mad. He kicked, hooked and bucked, twisting upside down and sideways, and just generally raised hell until we got a rope on him and snubbed him up to the side. He'd dented the roof, bent the divider gate, and kicked four of the wood slats on the side clean out. The old cow was pretty bad herself. She kicked everything in sight, and broke every wood slat she could reach.

The ride to town wasn't exactly a pleasure trip, either. Pappy was more than a little upset that these idiots had torn his good trailer near down to the axles. He took to cussing so much the air started turning blue. Some of those words I didn't even know. I was glad we didn't have to go no farther than Mineral Wells.

We were almost to the sale barn, rounding a curve, when this motorcycle cruised up alongside us and spooked the cattle. They started jumping around, trying to get away from that noisy thing, and that dang trailer spun us sideways in the street. One of the cow's hind legs was sticking out through the broken slats, so we had to take care of that before she broke it. While we were out there working, a teenager in an orange Volkswagen Beetle pulled up and started honking his horn.

"Hey you old fart!" he hollered at Pappy. "Get that wreck off the street."

Pappy just snapped. In three steps he was on top of that car. He pulled that smart-ass out through the window and half killed him before he could get away.

"Help!" the kid hollered, running around the other side of his car. "Help! The old man is crazy."

Pappy started chasing him and cussing for all he was worth, while Orville and me watched the show, which was about as funny a thing as we had seen in a long time. About the time we got the cow's leg back in the trailer, Pappy finally ran out of wind.

"If you value your life," he sputtered — he was bent over with his hands on his knees and blowing like a horse — "You had better get the hell out of here . . . real sudden like."

All that boy needed was a chance and he was gone. Pappy staggered back to the trailer, winded and face red as a chili pepper. He told us in no uncertain terms that, if we said one word, he would shoot us graveyard dead. I glanced at the gun rack in the back of his cab and took heed, but there was no way Orville could keep from laughing. Lucky for him, Pappy was on the other side of the pickup and couldn't see him.

"Get in the truck and shut up!" Pappy growled. "We've got to get these cattle to the sale before we get in any more trouble."

When we got back, Pappy's wife, Dixie, came running. She heard him cussing before we got out of the truck and was curious to know what was going on. He was still grumpy as a bear.

"Glad you're home, Pappy." She gave him a big hug around the neck. "How did everything go?"

Pappy started walking over to the stables. When he didn't answer, she turned to us.

"Do you know what's eating my old man?"

"We'll tell you later," I promised. "But it might be a good idea not to mention anything about the trailer, or hauling cattle or anything like that."

"Okay. I'll just take your word for it. What have you boys been eating, anyway? Pork 'n' beans?"

"How'd you know?" Orville gave her a puzzled look.

"I know cowboys," she said. "How about a hot meal tonight?"

I looked over at Orville, and for a minute I thought he was going to hug her neck.

After we unhooked the trailer and washed up in the stock tank, we drove up to the house. We had to circle the driveway twice before we got Ole Blue stopped, but she finally came to rest up against a stump.

"You all come on in this way," Dixie hollered at us from the kitchen door out back of the house.

When we went in the kitchen, I noticed a young woman, about my age, standing at the stove stirring a pan of gravy. Orville got a big smile on his face.

"Hi there, Sue," he said real cheerful like.

I knew that name sounded familiar. It was Pappy's daughter — the one Orville had told me about. She turned and glared at him and the temperature in there dropped forty degrees. But it didn't seem to bother Orville none. He strutted right over and gave her a peck on the cheek.

Somehow I knew this gal was not going to be as forgiving as her folks were. There was something about

77

her. I couldn't put my finger on it, but I swear, if she had stuck her tongue out, it would have been forked.

Now, I had been around women enough to know that a lot of them are kind of territorial when it comes to the kitchen, and Sue was no exception — maybe even a little more so. When Orville walked up and stuck his finger in the skillet, I started to get nervous.

"This would be pretty good if you put some more seasoning in it."

She didn't say a word; just sneered at him.

Orville laughed. He never was too quick at catching on. I, on the other hand, was headed for the door. Wasn't any sense both of us getting killed. I opened it enough so I could run, but I just had to see what she was going to hit him with. I hoped it wasn't that big iron skillet, because it was full of gravy, and I sure like gravy.

"Orville," Dixie said, "You're still as big a tease as you always was."

While her and Orville was carrying on, I spotted the sharp knife I was sure Sue was fixing to use to slit Orville's throat. I looked over at Pappy. He had been real quiet, sitting there with his eyes shifting back and forth sort of nervous like. I think he was looking for a place to hide, too.

"You boys sit down," he said to me and Orville. "Let's have some supper."

Orville, being slow as he is, picked the chair near the stove. I sat next to the door with my chair pointed sideways so I could make a break for it when things blew up — and I knew they would.

Orville started telling jokes and teasing Sue, but she never said a word. She carried the biscuits and chicken-fried steak over to the table. He took three biscuits and a piece of meat before the plates hit the table. Orville was a real chow-hound. Sue sat a big bowl of gravy right beside him and he proceeded to pour gravy over his biscuits and everything else on his plate. He took a big hunk out of one of the biscuits and was about to slam-dunk another when he let out a holler. He reached for the big mason jar of iced tea in front of him, tipped it up as fast as he could, and spit it back out even quicker, spraying tea all over the table.

Sue neglected to tell him she had poured a whole box of chili powder in the gravy — and a shakerful of salt in the tea. That woman was silent and deadly!

Pappy and I jumped out of Orville's way and Dixie looked on in horror as he started running around the table with Sue hot on his trail. He was still trying to catch his breath when he came around the second time. That's when she hit him on the head with a saucepan. It sounded like a machine gun — rat-a-tat-tat. It probably didn't hurt too much, because Orville is pretty thick-headed, but he wasn't going to stand there and let her do it again. He made a run for the door and Sue tripped him. When he hit the floor she was right there, whaling on him with that pan and screaming like a scalded cat.

"Have you had enough seasoning yet, funny man? Leave me high and dry, will you! You bum!"

While Orville was trying to crawl out the door and make his getaway, me and Pappy tried our best to look invisible. I was glad Dixie was there. She was the only one able to handle the situation. When she got a hold of Sue and pulled her off Orville's back, he shot out that door like a cannon.

But that girl was still on the warpath. I just knew she was wanting to hit on something — or some body — and

I didn't feel like getting my bell rung for something that knot-headed partner of mine had stirred up. So, I decided to get the hell out of there. And I didn't waste any time. In fact, when I went tearing out that door I dang near ran over Orville. He was still on all fours, throwing dirt and trying to gather momentum. I reached down and grabbed his collar and drug him to his feet. We hit Ole Blue at a dead run. I didn't even try to open the door — just dove in through the window and hit the starter. That old DeSoto had never moved so fast, and probably never did again, come to think of it.

When Orville straightened up in the seat I swear his eyes were still spinning from the banging he'd taken on his head. He wasn't talking real good either. After that dose of chili powder and salt tea, the words just sort of whizzed out of his mouth.

"What the hell touched her off?"

I couldn't believe he had said that. But one look at his face and I knew he didn't have a clue.

"Orville, you're too dumb to live without someone to feed you. Why in the world did you go in there blowing smoke like that?"

"I was only funning her, Hoss. How was I to know she'd come uncorked like that? Man, that woman ain't wrapped too tight. I mean, anyone who would deliberately ruin a whole pan of good gravy has got to be running with one wheel on the curb."

I looked at him in total disbelief. He had just got his butt kicked by a woman, and he's mad because she ruined the gravy.

"I know a man can survive on cold pork 'n' beans if he has to, but I surely do wish we had gotten to at least eat some of those good groceries. Thanks to you, that ain't gonna happen."

We drove a mile or so without saying anything. I was thinking about how good those biscuits looked when Orville piped up again.

"Turn this thing around, Hoss. I'm gonna go back there and tell Sue a thing or two."

"Hold everything!" I shouted. "How dense are you, Orville? Do you want that gal to finish what she started? She's plum serious about putting some hurt on you. You go back now and the odds are real good she's gonna blow a hole through you. And me, too, probably — just because I know you."

I could see he was trying real hard to think about what I had said. Thinking was a challenge for Orville.

"You might have a point, Hoss. Maybe it would be a good idee to lay low and let her cool down some. Dang, she's cute when she's mad, though. Ain't she?"

"If you say so. One thing's for sure. After fighting Sue off, capturing Bubba ought to be a breeze."

Next morning early, before the cattle realized we were anywhere in the country, we slipped up on a couple of cows and dropped a loop on both of them. We didn't give them a chance to untrack.

The cow Orville roped had a calf, and when she took to squalling, her baby kept popping in and out of the brush trying to figure out what was wrong with his momma. I tied off my cow, borrowed Orville's spare rope and rode into the shadows where the calf couldn't see me. While I waited for the little fella to pop out again, Orville was dragging his momma all around the clearing. She was making a hell of a fuss, and when the calf eased out of the brush to see where she was, I dabbed a loop on him before he knew what was happening. I started dragging him back towards the stable and, brother, was he bawling and carrying on, which turned out to be in our favor because his momma took right into following him. We snaked those two back to the stables in nothing flat, got them put up, and went back and picked up the other cow. We had all three of them in the round pen before seven o'clock.

"Hey, Orville," I said as I brushed the dust off my hat, "Not bad for a morning's work. Maybe we're getting the hang of this brush poppin."

Pappy was impressed to see the cattle in the pen.

"Well, looky here. Seems all you need to make a hand, Orville, was have a woman bang a pan off your thick skull. Must have knocked some rust loose."

Orville rubbed his head.

"Pappy, I can't figure out what Sue is so dad-blame mad about."

Pappy stuck a big wad of tobacco in his mouth and turned to me mumbling.

"That boy is dumb as a rock, ain't he?"

"Well, just think," I smiled, "If he hadn't run off two years ago, he might have been your son-in-law — in which case you'd have a pack of grandkids, and every one of the them dumber than he is."

He stood there like someone had just hit him between the eyes with a hammer. Then he spit, shook his head and glared at Orville.

"Damn! I wouldn't wish that on my worst enemy. Bet I wouldn't have suffered too long, though. If Sue didn't kill him first, I'd probably shoot the whole dang bunch — and get a medal for it."

Orville was busy making some adjustments to Ole Blue's headlight, so he hadn't heard our pow-wow. He came over and asked Pappy what had happened after dinner the night before.

Damned if I know," Pappy scowled. "There was so much hell-raising going on I left and went to town. When those women get stirred up like that, I get about as far gone as I can get."

Orville cocked his hat to one side and said: "Maybe I ought to go on up to the house and smooth things over."

Pappy might near jumped out of his skin.

"I sure wouldn't do that if I were you. Not just yet."

I grabbed my partner by the scruff of the neck and pointed him towards our horses. It was time we were getting back to work, I told him.

Our technique was improving. We didn't see a sign of Bubba, but four days later we had caught five more head of cattle. After that, they started wising up and heading farther north on the base. We figured that's where Bubba was, too. It didn't get any easier. The hills got steeper and the brush thornier. We hunted for three more days. We were beat, and so were our horses. It was time for a new plan.

Since we hadn't had a chance to spend any of the money we got from selling the first batch of cattle, it seemed like a good time to take a break. With a little jingle in our pockets we could at least buy some smokes and a bottle of hooch. The rest we could blow on foolishness like clothes, food — and maybe brakes for Ole Blue.

The first thing I did was buy a new hat. My old sombrero was never the same after the hooking that old cow gave it. The gal at the store in town gave me a real good deal on the new lid, so I still had plenty of money left to party with. That was a bad sign. Cowboys with change in their pockets always means trouble. Money's made to throw up in the air and run out from under it. I guess we just can't stand prosperity.

It was coming up on the weekend so we decided cow-catching could wait and headed for the honky-tonks on Jacksborough Highway out of Forth Worth. We had heard they were wild joints on Friday night — just our kind of place. Well, the dance halls were jumping and we didn't know which one to start with. Then we saw two old boys having one hell of a fist fight in the parking lot of the Studs and Steers. We knew we were home for sure. And it got better. That place was just plum full of good-looking women. We baled right in like we was trying to catch up on lost time. I spotted a couple of gals right off, sitting at a table all by themselves. That was a good sign. I collared Orville and we headed their way. Upon closer inspection, I saw that one of them was a knock-out, and the other might do in a pinch. So, I slid in beside the knock-out, Sherri, and left her sister Terri for Orville. She had on a blue dress, so I knew he wouldn't complain.

"Ladies," he said, "We hear it's a law here in Texas that if two cowboys show up and want to party, dance and just generally have a good time, it is your civic duty to see to it that they aren't disappointed."

The girls looked at Orville and then at each other and started laughing.

"You two sure are bold," Terri giggled.

"That's us. Bold!" said Orville as he snaked an arm around Terri's shoulder. "Would you like a drink?"

After a round of drinks, we were fast on our way to

convincing the girls that they were lucky to have stumbled onto two such charming guys. And the way Sherri kept staring at me, I was sure she was admiring my blue eyes.

"What happened to your face?" she said at last. "You been in a fight?"

At that point it was real tempting to say yes and dazzle her with one of my famous narrations — like a heartfelt tale of male chivalry gone sour and the resulting battle. But I decided not to steal any of Orville's thunder. For a change, I told the truth.

"No, we've been brush poppin."

The girls looked at each other again, puzzled.

"What's that, brush poppin?" Terri asked.

"I don't want to hear about it if it's something nasty," Sherri said.

"Well then," I smiled, "You'll be relieved to know that it just means we've been rounding up cattle in some sure-enough rough country."

"Oh!" they both squealed.

"We're from Kansas City," said Sherri.

"And we've always wanted to meet some real cowboys," her sister chimed in.

"You're in luck, girls. Me and ole Orville here are two of the very best cowboys there are . . . Well, maybe not the *very* best, but certainly in the top ten, 'cause all the other fellas send us fan letters."

Sherri scooted her chair closer to mine.

"Ooh, keep talking. I just love your accent."

That's all the encouragement we needed. Mark Twain couldn't spin a yarn any better than me and Orville. We told stories that made Wild Bill Hickok and Buffalo Bill look like Sunday school teachers. Of course, the more we drank the wilder the stories got, and the wilder the stories got, the closer Sherri and Terri got to us. It was a fine arrangement, and it was about to get better.

Sherri leaned over and put her hand on my thigh.

"Have you ever been to Mexico?"

Well, I just couldn't help myself. At that moment I would have claimed to be Poncho Villa himself if it meant holding Sherri's interest.

"Oh yea," I winked at my partner. "Me and Orville worked on a ranch right on the Mexican border. We had to carry guns all the time on that place to fight off the renegade Indians and Mexican bandits."

Sherri leaned a little closer. She had on a real tight V-neck sweater and I swear, the more excited she got, that Vee got deeper and the sweater got tighter.

"No kidding! Are there really still Indians and Mexican bandits in Mexico?"

"Oh sure. Everybody knows that. When they captured Geronimo all his people stayed hid out in the mountains for years. Never let anybody see them."

"Geronimo?" Terri looked me straight in the eye.

"Yea!" Orville said. "You've heard of Geronimo, ain't you?"

The girls exchanged glances with each other and cackled like a couple of hens.

"Yea, I think so," Terri said, tossing her head back and grinning at me.

I went right on with my story.

"Anyway, once in awhile if they need horses, guns or ammunition, or something, they sneak over the border and steal it from the ranch. Then they go back and hide in the mountains. Those mountains are real rough. Most cowboys won't follow them, because if you go in, chances are you wont come out. And the Mexicans say there's a ghost in there that kills people. They won't even go near those mountains."

Sheri let out a little gasp, jumped, and landed right on my lap.

"Ooh, that's scary!"

I just couldn't stop myself.

"Now, those wild Indians try real hard not to be seen because they don't want anyone to know that there's still wild Apaches living free. If they even think you saw them, they'd kill you so you couldn't tell anyone else."

Sherri let out another gasp, put both arms around my neck and pulled my face to her chest. I could barely breathe, she was squeezing me so tight. But then, I wasn't sure I really needed to breathe too much anyway.

Meanwhile, Terri had snuggled up next to Orville like white on rice.

"Me and ole Orville here rode across five of them Indians one night and they started shooting at us. Then, well . . . did either of you gals ever see that movie True Grit with John Wayne?"

They both nodded.

"You know at the end where he rides toward all those outlaws with a six-shooter in one hand and a rifle in the other? Just riding and a-shooting? Well, they got that idea from Orville here."

Orville was so shook when he heard that, I think he almost sobered up.

"Is that right, Orville?" Terri squealed.

"Ye-eeah!" He nodded as she pinched his cheek.

"Yes sir! Orville shot three of them. I saw it with my

own two eyes. I got one myself, too. I don't think we killed any of them, because they rode off. But we sure hit them. We found blood the next day."

"Oh, how gory!" Sherri shivered. "Did you go tell the sheriff?"

"Naw. Orville here didn't want any publicity, so we didn't tell anybody except . . . well, Orville is personal friends with John Wayne so he wrote and told him all about it. Didn't you, Orville?"

My partner was beginning to look like one of those little dogs you see in the rear window of a car. Every time he heard his name, his head started bobbing.

"Go ahead, Orville," I said. "Tell them how the Indians sent their bravest warriors back to get revenge."

Orville had a good excuse for being slow. He'd been bucked off on his head too many times. I could tell he was trying to think up some scenes from one of those old movies he'd watched. It had to be a movie because Orville never read books. Fact is, I'm not real sure he could. When he started telling the plot of another famous movie with him as the hero, I was sure the girls would catch on. But they were even slower than Orville. Or maybe they hadn't seen the same movies we had.

"Ooh, Orville. Tell us how you rescued those poor women and children."

After a couple of hours of storytelling, Orville's head was bobbing every which way. I guess the girls never thought that to have done everything we told them about, we would never have had time to eat or sleep. And we'd probably be about seventy. But as long as they were listening, we kept telling the tales, which were getting to be downright ridiculous. About the time Orville was describing how he fought off three dozen Indians single-handed, he started to mumble and his words just weren't making sense anymore.

"Orville, what's the matter, Sugar?" Terri said.

Not wanting my buddy to embarrass himself, I answered for him.

"Orville was shot in the head during that raid," I spoke in a serious tone of voice. "Now, when he gets to drinking a little, his old brain goes tilt sometimes."

When the girls exclaimed what a brave little soldier he was, Orville got that big silly grin on his face and spilled half his beer on his blue shirt. That's when the pointing and grunting started.

When Orville got drunk, he lost all capacity to communicate in any kind of intelligent manner. All he could do was point and grunt. Like this one time when he was sitting in my pickup, drinking and generally minding his own business, and a cop walked up. He asked Orville what he was doing. Orville pointed and grunted. Then he asked where he was from, and Orville grunted and pointed. Thinking this was just another cowboy trying to be funny, the officer started to lose his patience, so I walked over and explained that my brother was mentally retarded. The cop walked off, Orville grunted, and then hit me in the eye with his pointing finger.

Now, I didn't mind that the girls were concerned over my partner's misfortune, but when Sherri got off my lap and went over to pet his bullet hole scar, I knew I'd given Orville just a little too much credit.

"I got shot, too," I said.

"Ooh, where?" Sherri wanted to know.

I unbuckled my belt. I was about to drop my pants

and show her, and that's when the fight broke out. It started with two young guys, but thirty seconds later everyone in the bar was turning it upside down. Even the women got in on it. Fact is, it was a big ole red-headed broad that got knocked into our table and spilled our drinks. That was the break we had been waiting for. Shoving a woman around, wasn't exactly good manners, but wasting good liquor was a sin. Besides, it was another chance to impress the girls.

We baled right into the middle of the ruckus and were having a high old time when someone yelled out that the cops were coming. We broke for the back door, grabbing the girls as we went. The parking lot looked a whole lot safer than inside that saloon. The girls tore out that door like they'd just seen a ghost and we were right behind them. Neither Orville or me was eager to get mixed up with the law.

"Say," I said to the girls when we got outside by the car, "Orville and me don't have to be back to the ranch until morning. Want to party all night?"

"There's nothing I'd rather do," Terri said.

"Gentlemen . . ," Sherri began.

I turned around to see if someone else had walked up behind us. I was sure she wasn't talking to Orville and me. But, she was talking to us all right . . . two of the best bandito-fighting Indian hunters that ever lived!

"Terri, we have to head back to Kansas City," said Sherri to her sister.

"Right now?" Orville managed to ask.

"Pretty soon. We're starting up our own business and if we aren't there on Monday to sign the papers, we'll lose the deal."

"What kind of business?" I asked.

"Well now, why don't you two just come up some time and we'll tell you all about it," she said

"That was a tempting invitation. So, Terri and Sherri were a lot more knowledgeable about the history of the old west and, as for me and Orville, we were looking forward to a future road trip to Kansas City.

We hit a couple more bars on the way back, so on Sunday we were both a little more hungover than usual. It took us all day to rest up, but when Pappy met us at the stables Monday morning we were ready to resume our cattle catching.

"Boys, I got a visit from the base's head honcho. He wants to know how the bull hunt is progressing. I told him we'd managed to capture quite a few cattle but he was only interested in that ole bull. He don't mind weeding as many cattle out of the brush as we can, but he says that bull's got to go. He can't hardly get his troops to stand watches since that jeep got demolished."

Orville cocked his hat to one side like he always did when he was fixing to blow some smoke.

"Pappy, we're going to get that bull all right. Ain't a critter ever been born that could get the best of me."

"That's real encouraging, Orville, seeing's how you can't even escape from my little ole whisp of a daughter beating on your noggin. Come to think of it, maybe I ought to send her out there with you two."

That's when I had to speak up.

"Please, Pappy. Don't do that. You know as well as I do that Sue would rather thump another skillet on his head than go on a shopping spree. And I'd get the after-shock for sure."

"You're sure-enough right about that, Dan."

Orville kicked the dirt, disappointed at our lack of faith in him.

"When you two are finished jawing, me and Hoss got a bull to catch."

"I'm impressed with your ambition, Orville, but by the looks of you, I'm not sure either one of you is up to chasing cattle today. Where have you boys been the past two days?"

"We'll have to tell you some other time, Pappy," I said. "I don't think your heart could stand it right now. Just give us a minute or two to finish off this here can of Texas caviar and we'll be ready to ride."

We gobbled down our beans and went to check on our horses. I was glad to see that the swelling in my pony's knee had gone. I was going to need a horse with some size and speed, and most important of all, a lot of heart.

We cut trail on some cattle but didn't see any tracks big enough for Bubba. After looking all day, we figured he was either holed up in the brush somewhere, or he had moved again. That base sure covered a lot of territory, and I was beginning to think we might never catch him.

"I don't know how in the hell we're going to find that dang bull," I said to Orville. "This base is as big as the XIT Ranch."

Orville scratched his head.

"Maybe we could get some of them helicopter pilots to help us locate him," he said.

Orville wasn't famous for coming up with good, or even mediocre ideas, but this one wasn't half bad.

"Sounds all right to me. Let's go and see what Pappy thinks about it."

Pappy was sucking on a cold beer when we got back to the stables.

"Say, Pappy," Orville said, "We ain't seen hide nor hair of that beast today. Do you suppose we could get some helicopters to help us out?"

"Good idea, Orville! I'll give the commander a call. God knows those boys don't have anything else to do."

Before the commander got there the next morning, a huge crowd had gathered at the stables. Word had gotten out that there was going to be a big cow hunt, and the troops who had boarded horses at the stables couldn't wait to be cowboys for a day. They were warting the hell out of me and Orville, stumbling around begging us to let them help, and then pestering us to show them what to do. That was the last thing we needed — a bunch of greenhorns getting in the way — or worse, maybe getting us killed. I pulled Pappy aside the first chance I got.

"Pappy, we want all these weekend cowboys out of here before someone gets hurt."

"Aw heck! Let them tag along. Those soldier boys could use a little excitement in their lives. Besides, this way you'll have some witnesses for your daring escapades."

Orville's eyes lit up like two flashbulbs. He always did like an audience.

"Hoss, I believe I better go over and give them fellas a few pointers."

I knew exactly what he was up to. He was going to show off and act like a bigshot. Well, he sure had his work cut out for him. Those troops had armed themselves with every excuse for a rope I'd ever seen. One guy had part of a clothesline, and another had an anchor line off a navy ship. It was so heavy he could hardly pick it up.

"Do you think that rope's big enough?" I asked.

"I heard that Bubba is the biggest damn bull that ever lived," he said. "I sure don't want my rope to break when I capture him."

"Well, I'll bet even money he wouldn't break that cable. Might jerk the saddle horn out of the tree, but I'm pretty sure your rope won't break."

He smiled real big like he was the smartest chicken in the coop.

Meanwhile, Orville had set a dummy on a bale of hay and had all his trainees lined up waiting to take a swing at it. Orville wasn't too bright, but he was sure enough a hand with a rope. He was having a ball showing off to those dudes and they were loving every minute of it.

The fella with the boat rope tried heaving it at the bale and hit one of his buddies in the head. Damn near knocked him cold. It was plum dangerous being anywhere near that crew. Even Orville had to protect himself. He stood behind a post and only looked out long enough to holler "Throw!" Then he'd duck back behind the post. Nobody knew which direction those ropes would fly when those boys turned them loose. They were about to whip each other to death when Orville stopped them for some more instructions. I figured he was probably wasting his time. Hell, they might not be able to rope Bubba, but they could sure enough club him into a coma.

In spite of all the practicing, there was no evidence of any improvement, so Orville finally lined the troops up like a bunch of school kids and told them to pay attention while he demonstrated one more time. They sure were a sight! What those boys lacked in roping skills, didn't even come close to making up for in fashion sense. They had the damnedest excuses for clothes. I guess they must have hit every store downtown. And I'll bet them store owners got rid of all their old things that nobody else would buy. They had the sorriest hats. Some of the brims were eight inches wide and the crowns were at least that tall, or taller. None of them fit. They were either too big or too little, and if some of those boys hadn't had such big ears their hats would have been down around their shoulders. One guy's bonnet sat clear on top of his head like a beany with a little string tied under his chin. And the boy standing next to him was wearing one as big as a rain barrel. To keep it from falling off, he'd poked a couple holes in the crown, run a shoestring under his chin and up over the top, and then tied it in a bow. Didn't make no difference, though. It still kept slipping. The only way he could see was to tilt his head back and peer down his nose. But the silliest of all had to be the guy with the sombrero — one of those wooden ones from Mexico that's supposed to hang on the wall. It fell off just about every time he moved. After it hit the dirt three or four times, he still didn't give up on it, even with half the brim broke off.

They all had high-water pants on, too, revealing an interesting assortment of footwear. I don't have a clue where they found some of those boots, but I guessed it was the five-and-dime store — the same place they bought their Roy Rogers spurs.

Yes sir, this crew was decked out for the last round-up, and Pappy was looking real prosperous, being's he had rented every horse on the base.

"Pappy," I said when I saw him stuff a wad of bills in his shirt pocket. "You got it out for a couple of those fellas? That paint and that old bay horse there ain't been rode but two or three times. And that was in the round pen. If they get out there in the open country they'll run off for sure."

"Naw, I think they'll stick with the rest of the horses. They all bunch up anyway."

"Well, even if they don't run, I'll bet they buck them dudes off before we get anywhere near that bull."

"So? They said they wanted something with a lot of spunk. I just give the customers what they want."

About then the commander showed up with a couple of pilots and two MP's in another jeep.

"Now, if you'll just explain to my pilots what you want them to do, we'll get started. We got a radio in this jeep so we can stay in contact with the helicopters. We'll locate that bull and then your boys can go ahead and do what they do best. Remember, we got to get that bull. I don't care about those old cows. The bull is our number one priority."

Orville and me described Bubba to the pilots and told them our plan. They had a chuckle about the bull's nickname, then one of the MP's pushed up the his helmet. He looked real familiar.

"Hi, I'm Jeffrey. Remember? From the bar. You drew this picture for me."

He removed a napkin from his pocket, spread it out on the hood of the jeep and proceeded to tell his buddy how much he knew about catching a bull.

"Betcha didn't think I'd remember all that," he said to me with a big smile.

If I had looked straight at him right then I would have cracked up, so I stared at the ground instead.

"Sure I did!" I said, shuffling my feet a bit. "That's

exactly right, Jeffrey. Now, why don't you two go on up where we saw that bull last and we'll be right along."

He folded the napkin nice and neat, shoved it in his jacket pocket, and the two of them took off in the jeep. When I turned around, there was Pappy, grinning like he'd just heard a real good joke.

"Hoss, I've seen some pretty cold-blooded things in my life, but this tops them all. You could get that kid killed, you know."

"Naw! When you're that dumb you don't ever get killed. A little bent, maybe."

"I believe I'll be keeping a closer eye on you from now on," he muttered as he climbed into the commander's jeep.

Orville and me saddled up and headed out, leaving Pappy and the commander to discuss the details of our battle plan.

"Did you bring the flags?" Orville asked.

"What are you talking about?"

"Well, we're leading the parade, ain't we?"

I turned around and, sure enough, there were about twenty horses strung out behind us. All those weekend cowboys were following us, jabbering away and having a high old time.

"We damn sure ain't gonna sneak up on anything with that crew along," Orville laughed.

When we caught up to Jeffrey's jeep, he was busy talking to the pilots.

"Are you sure you're up to this hunt?" Orville asked him.

"You bet I am! I can't wait to run into that jeep-wrecking son-of-a-bitch again."

I was thinking about what Pappy had said. Maybe someone that dumb did deserve at least a warning.

"Ain't you scared he'll tear up this jeep, too?"

"Are you kidding?" Jeffrey laughed. "I'm not scared — not since you guys showed me how to knock him out."

When Pappy and the commander drove up, we all reviewed our strategies and then Orville and me rode back and told all those idiots on the horses how they were to proceed. After the pilots drive Bubba into a clearing, we told them, it was their job to keep him there until we could get a rope on him.

"But if Bubba gets determined to go back in the brush," Orville said, "For God's sake get out of his way and let him go because he'll run clean over you."

About that time one of the pilots radioed Jeffrey that they had spotted the bull. When he asked for their location, one of the choppers rose high enough for us to spot it. They were about two miles away so we took off in that direction — Jeffrey and his sidekick in their jeep, me and Orville riding alongside them, and that bunch of good-for-nothing cowboys trailing behind.

One of the choppers made a few passes at Bubba, but he wasn't a bit scared of it. All he did was shake his head and paw the dirt. We had to come up with a better idea. As we approached the clearing, I told Jeffrey to ask the pilots if they could drive the bull out of the brush towards us.

"What was that you said?"

"Hand me that microphone," I said to Jeffrey. "Say, can you boys see any other cattle around?"

One pilot reported several head had been spotted

in a clearing off to the west of us.

"Do you think you can stir them up?" I asked.

"We can try."

"See if you can get them to running. Then push them over towards Bubba. Maybe he'll run with them."

"Okay. But we don't wanna get any closer to him than we have to. The commander would be mighty upset if he tore up these helicopters like he did the jeep."

"If you can steer those cows into the clearing, I think Bubba might follow them. It's about the only chance we got."

About twenty minutes later we could hear timber falling. The cattle were on the move and we were waiting, loops ready. We pulled our hats down low and took a deep seat. About half-a-dozen cows came crashing toward us, and Bubba wasn't too far behind. As soon as he broke out I jumped my horse right on him, swinging my loop.

Unfortunately, I just plain missed. I pulled out of the way to give Orville a shot. After all, Orville was the roper. I was used to being on top of them knotheads, not chasing them. Orville dropped his loop on ole Bubba, but instead of catching his head, he caught him deep, which was not so good. He dallied and tried to turn off but, because he'd caught him too deep, it didn't turn the bull's head. When Bubba hit the end of that rope solid, it jerked Orville's horse to his knees and the rope snapped like baling twine. Bubba turned and charged, hooking Orville and his horse both out of the way like they were no more trouble than a pair of tumbleweeds.

Still annoyed, Bubba headed straight for Jeffrey's jeep. He hit her broadside at full speed, lifting two wheels off the ground and nearly turning it on its side. Jeffrey and the other MP ripped the canvas door right off it hinges trying to get out the other side. While his buddy scooted away on his hands and knees, screaming at the top of his lungs, Jeffrey managed to pull out his pistol. He stumbled to his feet and got his legs to pumping, then he started shooting as he ran — not at Bubba — but at anything in his path.

I had been satisfied to sit and watch this whole wreck unfold, but when the lead went to flying, I wanted to run, too. Trouble is, the only place to go was back into the brush, and I just hated to do that. So I tried to get as small as I could in the saddle and stayed as far away from Jeffrey as possible. He finally ran out of bullets, and the last I saw of him he was hooking it out of there as fast as his legs would carry him.

Bubba was having a real party in that jeep. He had torn the top off, broke the windshield, bent the steering wheel and shredded the upholstery. He'd gone and drove one of those big horns into the passenger seat and when he jerked his head loose, the whole seat popped out. He looked pretty ridiculous standing there with that thing hanging off his horns, but one shake of those massive shoulders and that seat went sailing. He stood there pawing the ground, snorting and slinging snot like he was waiting for someone else to challenge him. I didn't know who he thought that might be, but it damn sure wasn't going to me, and by the looks of those other dudes, it wasn't going to be any of them, either. They were scrambling over each other to get away, their ropes and hats scattered for half a mile. I'll say one thing for them though, if the *Pony Express* ever makes a comeback, I reckon the whole bunch of them could hire on.

Bubba gave his big horns one last shake, and when he didn't see anything else worth tearing up, he trotted back into the brush. That ole boy knew he was bad, and was damn sure proud of it.

I rode over to catch Orville's horse. The poor thing was sweating and shaking, and I can't say as I blame him. If I had just been freight-trained by a ton of mad bull, I'd be shaking, too. In fact, I was shaking — just a little. Everything had happened so fast I hadn't had time to think. Now that things were considerably quieter, I got a big knot in my stomach remembering how close I had come to sudden death. If Orville hadn't dropped a loop on Bubba when he did, more than likely he would have come after me and sent me sailing the same way he'd tossed the seat out of that jeep.

I led the horse over to the mesquite tree Orville was clinging to. I couldn't see any arms or legs sticking out at odd angles, so I figured there couldn't be anything broke too bad.

"Hey Orville, you still think Ole Bubba is all blow and no go?"

As Orville unwrapped himself from the tree, he had more than a few words to say about Bubba — none of them you would consider complimentary — and then he started bad-mouthing helicopter pilots, Texas brush, and cowboying in general.

Orville didn't realize his horse had mashed his foot until he jumped up. He let out a bunch of words like I hadn't heard in quite awhile, and started hopping around in a circle, waving his arms and just a-cussing. Now, all this carrying on was real funny to me.

"That's a pretty cute little dance you're doing there.

101

I hope you remember it so you can show off next time we get to a dance hall."

That just made him madder. He started throwing rocks and twigs at me and, since I've always believed that sticks and stones *can* break your bones, I rode off to let him cool down a little. When I turned around, I saw him flop down on his butt in the dirt. He was looking over at the hole Bubba had knocked in the brush.

"Damn it! Where's my hat?" he growled. "Bring my horse back over here. I can't walk worth spit."

One thing I can say for Orville, he doesn't stay mad for long. Maybe that's got something to do with his short memory. Anyway, I led his horse over to him and helped him look for his hat.

"It's just not a good day when you get knocked clean out from under your sombrero," he said as he spotted his hat under a little mesquite tree about fifty yards from the one he'd been hanging onto when I found him.

I got off my horse, picked up his lid and handed it to him.

"Thanks, Hoss. Hey, what happened to everybody when Bubba broke loose? I guess I missed the show."

I told him everything, and when I got to the part about Jeffrey shooting up the place, he laughed so hard I thought he was going to hurt himself.

"You're gonna have to have a little talk with your roping students. Not a one of them took a swing at that bull. In fact, they weren't any help at all. Are your missing your rope? I saw Bubba dragging what was left of it into the brush. I'll just bet if you went in there and talked real sweet to him, Ole Bubba would let you take it back."

"I'll pass on that, Hoss. I believe I've had enough

excitement for one day."

Orville shifted in the saddle like every bone in his body was hurting.

"But if you were a true friend," he said, "You'd go get it for me."

"Hell, I wouldn't go in there if Sherri and Terri asked me to, let alone a scruffy-looking thing like you. You're best bet is one of them students — if you can find one. They all went to whipping and a-spurring when Bubba attacked the jeep."

"Let's go have a look at the damage."

Orville cringed when we rode up to what was left of the jeep. I got down off my horse to get a closer look and there on the ground was Jeffrey's paper napkin.

"Hey Orville, do you suppose Jeffrey was holding his directions in one hand and trying to punch Bubba with the other?"

"From what you told me, he was too busy trying to shoot him."

"Uh oh! Here comes the commander's jeep. He looks real mad. I think that's Jeffrey and the other MP in the back."

The commander's face turned purple when he saw that old jeep. He stomped and cussed as he worked his way around the wreckage, picking up a part every now and then and hurling it into the air. The soldiers were right behind him, trying to re-enact the whole fiasco, but he just didn't want to believe what he was seeing. He reached in to turn off the radio, which sounded like someone choking a chicken, then with the bent steering wheel in his hand, he started grinding his teeth.

Orville, trying to be his usual helpful self, picked up

a helmet off the ground and handed it to Jeffrey's partner.

"Here's your hard hat," he said.

"It's not a hard hat, it's a helmet, you idiot." Orville took offense.

"Pard, that sombrero of yours is a hat, and it's hard. So you can call it whatever you want, but to me it's a hard hat."

I walked over to Orville and reminded him how banged up he was. That's all we needed now was a fight to break out. I could just imagine the headlines in the newspaper: *Government and Civilians at War at Fort Walters.* When the commander saw us leaving, he looked at the jeep again and then yelled to me.

"That old son-of-a-bitch did it again, didn't he?"

"Yes sir, he did. But she didn't suffer much because," I pointed to Jeffrey, "Ole Wyatt Earp over there put a bullet in her and put her out of her misery."

When I showed the commander the hole in the hood, he marched over to Jeffrey and shoved his big old purple nose right in his face.

"Goddamn!" he said with his teeth clenched shut. "I *did* hear gunfire."

Jeffrey turned red as a beet and started sputtering something about line of duty, and that's when I decided to give him his napkin.

"Say, Wyatt, I found something of yours. You know, you should have used this. But, that's okay. I understand. They say the first time is always the hardest."

I stuck it in his pocket and walked past the commander, who finally saw something to laugh at. I could barely keep a straight face myself.

So, there ended the great bull hunt. By the time

104

Spring came I was back on the road again with my war bag, and so was Orville, although we went in separate directions. I like excitement as much as the next man, but Orville was a might too loco, even for me. As for Bubba, the Army put out a wanted poster — *Dead or Alive!*

After I left the base, I headed up Fort Worth way and run into an old boy who owned a wrecking yard. He wanted to know all about Bubba. Said he'd sure like to have him alive, because he figured he could wreck out cars cheaper than any man could. But last I heard, no one had seen hide nor hair of Bubba.

I heard a lot of other things, too. Pappy started driving a delivery truck for the Coors Brewing Company, and the commander retired and went back to the family ranch near Waco to raise sheep. Sold every cow on the place. Sue went to beauty school — after she got fired off her job as a short order cook. Jeffrey teaches hunter's safety classes somewhere in Arizona, and Sherri and Terri started up a catalog company in Kansas City. They sell marital aids. Might have to take them up on their offer and stop by and see them sometime.

As time went by, the Bubba legend continued to grow. I stopped at the Studs and Steers one evening and heard a kid who was stationed out at the base telling a civilian a hair-raising story about a beast out there that was half bull and half puma. He told how it had attacked and wrecked the Army's best helicopter, and plum scared everybody off the base, including the commander.

I wanted to interrupt him and tell the real story, because God knows the truth is story enough. But, what really got me is . . . he never even mentioned the two brave cowboys who led the hunt. Oh well!

THE HITCHHIKER

A rodeo cowboy spends a lot of time on the road getting from one show to another. There are some mighty pretty spots in this old country of ours, but from a cowboy's point of view, miles and miles of nothing in between. The trips weren't so bad when we traveled together because we were usually exhausted and slept most of the way — all except the driver that is, who usually stayed awake. But there were times when even he nodded off.

Occasionally I traveled alone, and I always hoped there would be something interesting to see to help me keep awake. Late one fall, in the morning about sunup, I was alone and on my way to a show in Colorado. I was somewhere between Clovis and Tucumcari, New Mexico, which is mostly ranch country, and it's a lo-o-o-ng way between mailboxes. I was dog-tired and so sleepy. Even the cold air wasn't keeping me very alert. So, I thought I'd fallen asleep and was dreaming when I saw a man wearing nothing but his under-shorts. He was standing in the middle of the road trying to flag me down. When I realized I was awake, I had a feeling that this might be just what I needed to keep me awake awhile longer, so I stopped.

The poor man was blue from the cold, and when he jumped into my truck he was shaking so bad he was rattling.

"Thank you! Thank you for stopping." He was barely able to stutter. "I was about to freeze to death out there."

I didn't question him. I just handed him the old blanket I kept behind the seat. He wrapped it around himself as tight as he could — so tight he looked like a burrito. His teeth were still partly clenched — or frozen together, I'm not sure which — but when he warmed up enough to talk, he introduced himself.

"Pleased to meet you, mister. My name is Bob. I'm from Texas."

That's all he could get out at first. He hunkered closer to the heater vent and looked like he would have crawled right in if he could have. I sure wanted to hear his story but I didn't rush him any. After a bit he tried to talk again.

"I'm a roughneck down around Midland. I just got off evening tower and my wife and I were taking off to do some hunting in the mountains round Cimarron. I was really tired from working so I crawled in the camper to get some sleep while my wife drove."

He was staring at my thermos.

"I don't have much coffee left and it's probably not too hot, but help yourself."

"Thank you, partner."

He poured out what was left and gulped it down, then held the cup in his hands next to his chest.

"I'm not sure what happened after that. Best I can figure my wife must have gotten sleepy and pulled off the road for a little nap. I was back there in the camper in my sleeping bag. When I woke up I had to pee. Guess I should've pulled my pants on but as bad as I had to go, and as cold as it was outside, I thought it would only take a few seconds. So I just hopped out and into the bushes right quick like."

He stopped and pulled the blanket up under his chin and shook his head.

107

"Anyway, I guess she woke up while I was in the weeds. I was standing there with nothing but a grip on myself when I heard the engine start up. She laid rubber taking out of there. Must've been trying to make up for lost time because she didn't even hear me holler."

I was trying my level best not to laugh but I just ain't that strong. I was holding my side with one hand and driving with the other, thinking about poor old Bob out there when she put her foot to the floor. He claimed he took off after her, but with no shoes he couldn't have outrun a one-legged fat man, let alone that pickup truck. I guess he was starting to warm up a little because even he had to chuckle a little at himself when he thought about how he must have looked.

"Say, could I have one of those smokes?"

"You betcha! Help yourself."

"I really just wanted to sit down, but I knew I'd freeze to death. Besides, my butt was so cold I was afraid if I sat on a rock I'd stick to it and never get loose. So I started walking, and in twenty minutes I was really cold. I tried to run around to build up some heat but between the rocks and stickers, and being barefooted, I couldn't even do that. I tried jumping up and down to generate a little heat. That's when I saw the lights of your truck coming up over the hill. I was never so glad to see anything in my life. I can't thank you enough, partner."

"You know, Bob," I laughed, "If I really step on it I think we can catch up with your wife."

I let the hammer down and off we went. I could tell old Bob was really tired, but I think he was too scared to go to sleep again. It was about fifty miles to Tucumcari, and just as we got to the outskirts of town he spotted his rig at a stop light. When I pulled up next to his pickup, he rolled his window down and hollered to his wife. She looked over and might near had a heart attack when she saw him.

There was a truck stop just ahead. Bob pointed to it and told her to pull over. Speechless, she just nodded and obeyed.

"When we get over there I'll get me some clothes on, and how about having some breakfast with us?"

I wouldn't have missed that conversation for a Bob Wills dance. When we pulled into the truck stop, Bob's wife jumped out with a look of total disbelief on her face.

"How in the world did you get in there?"

Old Bob was warmed up and his sense of humor began to show.

"This ole boy pulled up beside us and offered me a beer so I just naturally crawled over and got in his truck with him and had a beer."

I went along with Bob.

"That's right. Thirstiest man I ever did see. He just climbed out of that camper and into my truck like a monkey. We must have been doing sixty miles an hour, but he never weakened. You ought to know better than to put a man back there with no beer. He could have died of thirst."

She just stood there, mouth open and her head cocked to one side looking real puzzled. Bob, still in his underwear, a shade of pale blue with goosebumps the size of nickels, tried to look serious. I was about to bite a hole in my lip. Obviously something had happened but she wasn't buying our story.

"You lying son-of-a-bitch! I don't know what happened but that damn sure ain't it."

Bob gave her a hurt look.

"Now Tess, when have I ever lied to you?"

"I know you're lying because your mouth is moving. If you don't tell me what really happened I'm going to kick your blue butt all over this parking lot."

Tess was a hard woman. She was standing in front of the door to the camper, so Bob had to cooperate.

"Why don't you two go on inside and get a table," he grinned. "I'll grab my clothes and get dressed, and meet you inside. I'll tell you everything, Tess. I promise."

When she moved aside he jumped in that camper like there was a free barbecue in there. Then Tess turned to me and looked me square in the eye.

"Maybe you'd like to tell me what happened. I don't want no wild west story, either. Just what the hell is going on here?"

I thought the whole thing was pretty darn funny, so I smiled and said: "It's just like your husband said. He was thirsty."

"You're as big a liar as he is. I ought to just leave him with you."

This was fun. When Tess stomped off into the cafe I followed her and sat down. She glared at me across the booth, not saying a word. The waitress came over with coffee and asked if we wanted to order breakfast.

"There's going to be another idiot join us in a minute," Tess said as she stared out the window at their camper. "We'll order then."

The waitress just shrugged.

Tess still wasn't speaking to me. She was stirring her coffee so hard I thought she'd wear a hole in her cup. When she finally mumbled something about killing somebody, I wasn't sure if she was talking about me, Bob, or the both of us.

When the waitress looked at me for a sign, I winked and nodded toward Tess.

"Don't mind her. She hasn't had her medication yet."

Tess gave me a look that made the hair on the back of my neck stand up, and I was wishing ole Bob would hurry up and get in there.

"I don't know how you fit in or who you are, but I'm starting to take a strong disliking to you, so don't push it."

I was sure relieved when Bob came in and plopped down beside his darling wife.

"Zip your pants up before the whole world sees your shortcomings!"

Bob laughed and did as he was told.

"Hon, you seem a little testy this morning. Is something wrong?"

Tess couldn't take anymore.

"I started out this trip with my husband in the back of our camper asleep. The next thing I know he's in a truck that pulls up beside me . . . with someone I've never seen before that is as big a smart ass as he is. And both of you trying to give me a cock and bull story about jumping from one vehicle to another because you were thirsty. And you wonder why I'm testy?"

The fun was over. Tess was demanding an immediate answer.

"I'll promise you one thing. If you don't tell me what really happened, that deer rifle is going to be put to good use."

"Now, Hon, don't get mad. We was just having a little fun. The truth is, Dan here kept me from freezing to death. Back up the road a ways you stopped to take a little nap, I guess. Anyway, I woke up and had to answer mother nature's call. When I was in the weeds you took off and left me standing there in the middle of nowhere freezing my butt off till Dan here came along and rescued me."

"He was really something to see, jumping up and down in nothing but his under-shorts, waving his arms, trying to get me to stop. He woke me up from my nap. I wouldn't have passed him up for the world. I just had to find out how he managed to get in that predicament."

By this time Tess had lightened up considerably. In fact, she was laughing. She laughed so hard tears began to stream down her face, finally realizing that the joke really was on her husband and not her.

I figured it was about time for me to be getting back on the road, so I grabbed my jacket off the back of the booth and said my good-byes.

Bob picked up the ticket and insisted on paying for breakfast. When he got up to shake my hand and thank me, the tablecloth followed him, sending all the dirty dishes and silverware crashing to the floor. He just stood there dumbfounded, unaware that one corner of the tablecloth was zipped up in his fly.

"Woman!" he hollered to Tess who was shaking her head in disbelief. "Get in the truck. We're going home. The way my luck is running, if I went hunting I'd wind up shooting myself . . . or you!"

He was still trying to pull the tablecloth out of his pants as he headed toward the cash register.

"And I'm driving!"

112

NO SPEECHES ALLOWED

Being buddies is not something a cowboy takes lightly. We can be an ornery bunch to get along with, but believe it or not, we do have our own set of ethics.

One of the most important things is: cowboys stick together. I mean, if you only have enough money for one hamburger, you just split it. If an old boy comes along that can't afford a place to stay, you always let him throw his saddle blanket in your room, no matter how crowded it is. And if you only have one beer left, you let your buddy have a swig before you finish it off. When a fight breaks out, you bale in there even if you don't know the one who started it. When you go to a honky tonk and there's only one gal to dance with, you take turns dancing with her. Well, okay . . . maybe we don't go that far, but I'm sure you get the picture. Women are another topic altogether.

Whenever I ran with Larry, I had to constantly remind myself of the cowboy code of ethics, otherwise I would have had to shoot him to put both of us out of our misery. Every now and again you meet a couple of guys who are buddies and you just wonder how the heck that happened. Me and Larry were one of those pairs.

Back in the sixties we made some rodeos together, even though we couldn't get along worth a damn. Each of us knew he was the smartest, toughest, the best looking, the best bronc rider and, of course, that the other was as dumb as a fence post and couldn't ride a stick horse. We had one thing in common, though. As everyone knows, cowboys are prone to get into fisticuffs if things get a little too boring. And it wasn't unheard of for certain cowboys to start a fight just for the sheer fun of it. Larry and me fit the latter category. Neither of us needed an excuse to mix it up whenever it suited us.

It was common knowledge around home that I had never backed down from a fight in my life. But I did have enough sense — if I wasn't too drunk — not to try and whip a whole bar full of men by myself. Besides, I was a lover at heart. If there was a good-looking filly in the bar, I just might be so busy I would have no interest in fighting at all. Also, being a good storyteller gave me a distinct advantage. The best storytellers always get plenty of free drinks. And it wasn't unusual for a cowgirl to fall in love with a storyteller, for at least one night, anyway.

Larry, on the other hand, was half Indian, and tough as boot leather. He liked fighting. You just couldn't hurt him. The harder you hit him, the wilder he got, especially when he was drinking whiskey. Now, that in itself didn't cause trouble, but there was one thing about Larry that caused trouble to come calling on a fairly routine basis. He fancied himself somewhat of a politician. He figured he could solve most of the problems in this country if the powers-that-be would just listen to what he had to say. But like most self-professed politicians, Larry couldn't always find an attentive audience. By the time most of the other cowboys had settled down at their favorite watering holes, they just weren't too interested in politics of any sort. Larry, never having been one to recognize some of life's little subtleties, was awfully slow to figure that out. So, he'd just go on talking till someone threw the first punch.

Larry and me always seemed to attract considerable attention, both during and after a rodeo — like the time we left one show in Santa Fe and drove all night to get to another in some little town in Arizona. We had been on a lot of stock in the past three weeks, and we were dog-tired and sore. And since we were down to one meal a day and borrowing gas in the middle of the night, we were not in very good humor, either. It must have been ten or eleven o'clock when we pulled into a mining town about a hundred miles short of our destination.

Larry said: "Let's stop and get a beer or two. We've made good time and I need to stretch my legs."

Now, that didn't hurt my feelings any. In fact, it sounded like a pretty good idea. I was thirsty. So, we went into the Ole Mine Shaft bar. It was crowded because the swing shift from the mine was just getting off. Most of the people in the saloon were miners that had come to let off a little steam after a hard night's work. With a bar that was packed full, we knew we had a captive audience.

As soon as I found a place to sit, I went to telling my wild west stories. The drinks were coming about as fast as we could put them down, and the tequila started to take its toll on Larry. He began to pontificate about the importance of the American cowboy versus the significant lack of importance of the common miner in the building of our fine country. He was getting fired up, and the more he drank, the more his lack of diplomacy became apparent.

After awhile, one of the miners took offense to something Larry had said and told him so. Larry hit that guy one time and knocked him smooth out. But he didn't stop there.

"I always thought miners were tougher than that, but I can see you all are just a bunch of sissies." He took a big swallow of tequila, stuck out his chest and belched real loud. "Me and my buddy Dan here can whip every man in the house."

115

I sure hated to hear him say that. A cute little blonde named Sue Ellen had been snuggling up next to me and I thought sure she was falling in love. I took a quick look around the building, hoping I'd see another cowboy hat. When I didn't see any, I knew we were going to get hurt. I couldn't believe Larry was that stupid. Those guys had been underground most of the day, swinging picks and shovels and generally busting their butts. I just knew they were looking for an opportunity to get rid of their frustrations, and my buddy had obliged them.

I'm here to tell you, a peaceable storyteller like myself has no business hanging out with a politician like Larry. Thirty-to-two is not good odds, and those miners were tough men. Fists flew, tables collapsed, glasses broke, good whiskey spilled, but even though I knew Larry was dead wrong, and that I was about to get pulverized, I had to help my buddy, no matter how stupid he was. In the end Larry and me got our butts kicked. In fact, we got the hell beat out of us. I wasn't any too happy about it, but I had no choice. It's the cowboy code.

We didn't feel like any more excitement that night, so we headed straight for the rodeo and drove up to the arena first thing.

A bunch of our buddies were gathered around the chutes: Red, Harold, Jim, and a young kid I'd never seen before. All of them, except the boy, knew us pretty well. I'm sure our black puffy eyes, broken noses and torn ears came as no surprise to them. The kid, however, stared at us like his eyes were going to pop out.

"Hey, boys. Look!" Jim said. "It's the storyteller and his buddy, the politician."

They were all waiting for the "epic saga" — that's

116

what they called it when we went to relating one of our adventures. They just loved hearing about how much trouble we got ourselves into, and they could always count on me to give them a blow-by-blow report. I started the tale and when I got to the part about having to dump Sue Ellen to defend Larry, the kid interrupted me.

"That's the stupidest thing I ever heard," he said, his hands on his hips like he knew everything there was to know about everything. "Only a damn fool would leave a girl like that to get in a fight he didn't start."

The cowboys looked at him like he had two heads. That boy just didn't get it at all.

"Who's the new pup?" I asked.

"This here is Tye," Jim laughed. "Would you believe this is his first show?"

"That so," Larry said. "Son, you got a lot to learn about cowboys. And since I'm a wise and generous man, I'm going to take you with me to the next show."

Larry walked over and put his arm around his new traveling companion, but Tye ducked and took off running. When he figured he was out of Larry's reach, he turned around and yelled at him.

"I wouldn't go with you to the Cowboy Hall of Fame. You're nuts!"

Tye stayed plum away from all of us during that rodeo. I heard he did okay later in the pro's, but he never did have many friends. I guess he just never learned how to play well with others.

ENTRY FEES

There are worse things than being married to a cowboy, like . . . well, I'm sure there are worse things, but nobody would ever have convinced my wife, Waydene.

Waydene wasn't one to complain about much, except maybe my being gone for such long stretches when I was rodeoing. And maybe the fact we were broke most of the time. Come to think of it, she did mention on a few occasions that she was no nurse, and that it seemed like I sure was busted up a bunch.

I had good intentions, though. I admit I blew a lot of money before I got it to the bank, even when the bills were due, but I knew something my Waydene didn't. I knew if I could get to just one more rodeo, I was sure to win, and all our troubles would be over. I'm just telling you this so you'll be clear about why I done what I did, and why Waydene acted like a cow loose in a patch of loco weed.

In 1968 I was sure having a run of bad luck. I was so broke I couldn't pay attention, which is why I was so glad Waydene had a job. Unfortunately, she insisted on paying every single bill we had, so there wasn't anything left over for important things like entry fees. A big rodeo was coming up in July, not far from where we lived. I knew I was going to score big, but Waydene just wouldn't give in. No matter how much I begged and pleaded, she was stuck in neutral.

Now, I can't say that Waydene was mean. Quite the opposite. She was a good ole gal, but after years of waiting around for me to grow up and settle down, and

118

maybe stay home once in a while, she was just plain wore out. She was not about to give me money for entry fees that would send me down the road to another rodeo. She just kept talking about me getting a job. And every time she said that word I would get a little weak in the knees and start feeling like I needed to break for the bushes, pronto. I was just like all the other cowboys I knew — too lazy to work and too nervous to steal. Why would I get a forty-hour-a-week job when I could make more in eight seconds on top of a bull, and have fun, too? Anyway, while cowboy logic made perfect sense to me, Waydene and the rest of the wives tended to take a real dim view of our reasoning.

When Waydene told me flat out — no ifs, ands or buts — that she wasn't going to give me money for entry fees no matter what, I had to think of something quick. Now, maybe that was my downfall — the quick part, that is. I do my thinking better when I do it real slow like. I was pondering my dilemma, when I spied the new washer and dryer that Waydene had bought, and suddenly I had me one of those quick-thinking ideas. I wasted no time calling my buddy, Bill, to come over and help me get started with my plan.

Bill was always good about lending a buddy a hand, but he looked kind of nervous when I told him I needed help to load those appliances onto my truck so I could take them to the used furniture store.

"Dan, why on earth would Waydene want to go and sell a new washer and dryer she just bought?"

I told him about the entry fees and that it wasn't exactly her idea.

"Shoot! When she finds out, she's gonna blow a

hole straight through you, and there's not a jury in the world that would convict her if she did."

"I know all that, Bill. But she's gonna feel a whole lot different about it when I come home with my winnings. Hell, I'll have enough to buy an entire laundromat."

Bill just shook his head.

"Uh-huh! Well, I hope your luck gets a whole lot better than it's been these last few months. That's all I got to say."

Reluctantly, he agreed to help me, but only if I made a solemn vow not to tell Waydene about it.

After the deed was done, I called the rodeo and entered the bull riding. Then I took off down the road. I was drawed up for that night and sure enough relieved I had drawn a good money bull. I was the first one up, too, and I was sitting down on old Wet Hen when Bill, who was pulling the rope, heard a big commotion going on in the alley behind the chutes.

"What the hell is all the noise about?"

I turned around to see for myself. Out of the corner of my eye I saw cowboys running over each other to get out of the way of whatever it was that was coming down that alley. Of course, I figured one of the bulls was loose, and I was glad I was in the chute.

With cowboys scattering like a covey of quail, I just had to see what could possibly have scared them so bad. So, I pulled myself up to get a better view, and that's when I saw Waydene. She had a cattle prod in each hand and she was shooting fire at any cowboy that dared to get in her way. There wasn't one man brave enough to tell her to move on out of the alley. That woman was really p.o'd!

I had to admit she had a right to be mad, but she

wasn't just mad at me. She was plum disgusted with rodeos in general — rodeo announcers, rodeo clowns, bull doggers, team ropers, and just about anything that resembled a cowboy. Hell, I think she was even mad at Hank Williams!

Waydene was traveling fast, and any cowboy who didn't move faster than she was, why she'd just hit him with one of those hot-shots, sending enough juice through him to melt his belt buckle. All cowboys know, of course, that if a wife ever goes on the prod, you had better give her all the room she wants. Those ole boys were jumping like grasshoppers in a brush fire. And once they were out of her way, she had a clear path to me and Bill.

When Waydene saw Bill standing up on the chutes pulling a rope, she knew exactly where I was. I had just taken my wrap and was tied on the bull when she hit my partner. She got him with both prods, might near welding his hat to his head.

"Get out of there!" she screeched. "You probably helped him, you bum!"

There she was, standing right above me, and me tied on to one mean bull with nowhere to run. She sent a charge that went right through me and the bull, too.

"You sorry son-of-a-bitch! Steal my washer and dryer will you? I'll teach you a lesson that will finally get through that thick skull of yours."

She hit me again. That bull was about as unhappy with the whole affair as I was. He was getting upside down in the chute and mashing the hell out of my legs. I hollered for help.

"Damn, boys! Open the gate at least. Me and this ole bull got to have some relief real quick like."

121

As soon as they popped the latch, Wet Hen blew out of the gate and cranked it back to the left. He was spinning like a top and I was right in the middle of him, not moving an inch. I think I was glued to that rope. Meanwhile, Waydene was just getting started. She climbed over the chutes and ran out to the center of the arena with her weapons popping and crackling through the night air like she was a witch in an electric storm. But when she took to cursing me, that's when the air turned blue.

"Come on back, you coward! You'll think that bull rocked you to sleep and sung you a lullaby compared to what I'm going to do to you after you get off of him."

I was so scared you couldn't have pulled me off that bull with a winch truck. I tried to look gone, but she had me in her sights. There wasn't any chance of escape. I didn't have a prayer.

The crowd was dumbfounded, at least until they got the gist of what was going on. The women especially got excited and began to clap. Scared at first, the other cowboys just stood there with their mouths hanging open. But after they realized that it could have been them in my place, my little predicament just plum tickled them to death. So, they joined the rest of the crowd, laughing and cheering like Waydene was the main event.

I was definitely in no hurry to finish that ride. Before I knew it, the whistle blew and old Wet Hen slowed down. But I didn't get off. Even when he came to a complete standstill at the far end of the arena, I stayed on him. Both of our tongues were hanging out. We were exhausted. Waydene, on the other hand, had barely warmed up. She was at the other end of the arena hitting the buttons on her cattle prods and hollering in that cold voice she always got whenever she was really stirred up.

"Step off that bull and take your medicine, you thief. Right now!"

She hit those buttons again, sending a shower of blue sparks in my direction.

I sat on that bull and did what any cowboy would do when staring into the face of danger. I yelled for somebody — anybody — to save me. Things got grimmer. I knew no cowboy in his right mind was going to get in the way of that madwoman. Besides, they thought this was just about the funniest show on earth and they couldn't wait to see what was going to happen next.

Just when I was about to give up all hope — I had this vision of becoming the very first Kentucky fried cowboy — one of the pick-up men dropped a loop on Waydene and pinned her arms long enough for two cowboys to run out and take her prods away. She was still cussing me when they drug her out of the arena.

Relieved, I stepped off that old bull and started back to the chutes. As I crossed the arena on wobbly legs, the crowd started to applaud. I didn't know if it was the ride or Waydene's performance that caused them to clap so hard, but it wasn't long until it turned into a standing ovation. I looked up at all of them, removed my hat, and took a bow. In spite of their obvious approval, Waydene was still spitting fire when I got back to the chutes, even though she'd lost her hot-shots. All of my sensitive buddies were about to fall down laughing. They could hardly wait for the big confrontation. So, I got prepared for the final act. I eased up close enough to where Waydene could see me, but just out of her reach.

"Hey, Babe," I said. "Did you hear that score? I'm

gonna win this bull riding for sure. Hell, I probably got extra points for staying on so long, and I have you to thank for it."

That only made her madder. I can't repeat all the things she had to say, but she really lit into me.

"You low life . . . I worked my butt off to pay for that washer and dryer and you, you haven't put in a hard day's work since I met you. If you think all that whoopin' 'n' hollerin' out there is gonna make up for this, you got another think coming!"

I knew I was in serious trouble this time. I hung my head and tried to look hurt.

"But, Honey, I did it for you. Everything turned out just the way I planned."

Waydene stood there with a look on her face like someone had just dropped a brick on her head.

"Did it for me?" she screamed.

"Sure! I knew my luck was going to change. This rodeo has always been good to me, so I said to myself: self, go on and win that rodeo for Waydene and buy that sweet wife of yours a good washer and dryer — one of them fancy type that does everything but fold the clothes for her. Then, with what's left over, go pay off some bills so she won't have to work so hard."

I sort of cocked my head to one side and gave her one of my famous smiles. I was real proud of myself for coming up with such a believable story on such short notice. I damn near believed it myself, and I was just sure Waydene would.

First she gave me a cold, hard stare. Then she started laughing.

"You're so full of shit you stink! I don't believe one

lying word from your mouth."

"Aw, come on, Waydene."

But she wasn't done yet.

"It looks like you're gonna get some money for that ride. Well, I'm real glad, because I'm here to collect it. And I'm gonna see to it that you follow through on that little plan of yours. You know, the one where you're gonna buy me those fancy new appliances. I ain't gonna kill you today, but . . . if you ever even think of doing something like this again, I won't use a cattle prod, I'll use a shotgun. Is that clear you, knothead?"

I'm nobody's fool. I accepted my reprieve graciously. Meanwhile, Bill saw his chance to sneak off and was tiptoeing down the alley when Waydene spotted him.

"And as for you, jerk, if he ever does this again and you help him, I will personally nail your hide to the barn door. Is that understood?"

Bill didn't say a word. He just froze there, wide-eyed, trying to look innocent. Of course, he didn't fool Waydene for a minute.

I'd like to say that I never hit another streak of bad luck after that. But I like to stick as close to the truth as possible, and the truth is, I had some more rough times, like all cowboys do. One thing did change, though. To this day I get just a little weak in the knees every time I see a washer and dryer. And I can honestly say, I ain't never touched once since.

DON'T FORGET THE EGGS

When you're a rodeo cowboy, and living on the road, one of the last things you worry about is something to eat, that is, until the rumbling in your gut is so loud it scares the bull underneath you. Then eating becomes a priority. I'm here to tell you that if an opportunity arises to chow down heavy, you do it because you never know when you'll get a chance to fill up again.

Me and Roscoe, a bareback rider who hit the rodeo circuit with me during the sixties, hadn't made a dime for three weeks straight. That's the way it goes sometimes. Everyone hits dry spells. You just live with it. It was the summer of 1969 and we hadn't had a bite to eat in over a day, but we knew, if luck was with us, we'd have money sticking out of every pocket in a day or two. Since we were both real good at hustling, there was a pretty good chance we could come up with some groceries and a place to spend the night if we put our minds to it. All we had to do was find a rodeo.

Our next stop was Williams, Arizona. After paying our entry fees we didn't have a nickel left but we didn't care. We had both drawed up the next afternoon so we had plenty of time to take care of things like eating, sleeping and, of course, partying.

We hung around and watched the show the first day. No one made any high-scoring rides so it was still wide open, and all the other cowboys were near as broke as Roscoe and me. I figured they hadn't ate all day either, because the grumbling was getting just plain distracting. After awhile another bareback rider from Texas remembered he had some beef jerky stowed away in his war bag for emergencies. It wasn't much, but it at least filled the hollow spots until we could find something better.

Williams was a small town — just two bars — but it was a cowboy town, and the folks there sure liked to have a good time. When we got to the first bar, the dance had already started and everyone was having a high old time. Me and Roscoe ordered ourselves a couple of bottles of beer and leaned up against the bar while we looked the place over. About that time a couple of hippies who were passing through town walked up and stood in front of us. Now, I am usually friendly towards strangers, but back then there was something about long hair on a man that didn't set right with me, and I felt that I should let someone know my feelings about it.

"You know," I said like I was trying to be helpful, "The cowboys around here are real handy with their pocket knives, if you know what I mean. If you want to keep that long hair, maybe you had better get the hell out of Dodge."

When those two looked around the room, all they saw was a sea of hats. There wasn't another long-hair in the bunch. They took off so fast they forgot to pick up their change, which Roscoe slipped into his shirt pocket.

The old boy standing next to us tipped his worn-out Stetson in my direction and chuckled.

"That's the smartest thing those two boys have done all day. If they had stayed around here they sure enough would have got their manes roached."

He took a big swig and emptied his shot glass. That's when I noticed the rest of his outfit — starched dungarees, white tennis shoes and a pale-yellow shirt with

127

a button-down collar. None of it looked like it belonged to that hat.

"By the way," he said, "My name is Les. I used to be a dingy bull rider just like you boys when I was a might younger — and a whole lot dumber. But I got married and my wife made me quit about five years ago. You know how those gals feel about rodeo and such."

That explained the get-up he was wearing. At first I thought he was an insurance salesman, or a manager at Sears & Roebuck. But something about the way he held that shot glass made me think he really had been a bull rider once. Or maybe it was the way his short little legs bowed. Anyway, the comment about his wife brought up some memories I had been trying to forget, and I swear I got a tingle in my butt thinking about my own prod-wielding ex-wife. Roscoe had had a few experiences with the weaker sex, too. But I don't know that either one of us ever took to dressing funny because of it.

"You know," he continued "What I can't figure is, why she married me in the first place. She hates cowboys. Thinks we're a bunch of bums that never grew up."

"Hey, Dan," Roscoe grinned at me. "You sure he ain't talking about your old lady?"

"Sounds familiar," I agreed.

Figuring he had found him a pair of sympathetic friends, the old bull rider bought us a round of drinks.

"Why, she won't even let me wear boots. Says it's not sophisticated enough. But she has a lot of money and a big house. You know, every cowboy's dream . . ."

"What else could a man want!" Roscoe said as he drained his bottle of beer.

"I don't know about you two," I grinned, "But

my ideal woman is deaf, dumb, oversexed, and owns a liquor store."

Well, they thought that was pretty darn funny. They laughed till tears came to their eyes. But the truth is, at that particular point in my life, I really wouldn't have minded finding a rich woman with nothing better to do than spend money on me. As for Roscoe, it wasnt hard to tell what was on his mind.

"I had me a rich wife once," he said. "Couldn't cook worth a damn. Hell, she didn't even know how to boil water!"

Roscoe had been married seven times. Once he had told me he wanted to marry a woman from every state in the Southwest, and maybe a couple from the Midwest, too. Didn't want a Yankee gal, though, because they didn't know nothing about fried okra and cream gravy.

"And that wasn't the only problem," he continued, "She was ugly as a mud fence. That's what I got for following my pappy's advice. He told me: 'Son, always marry an ugly woman and you'll be glad when she leaves you.' That part was right enough, but it's too damn bad she didn't leave some of her money when she took off with that damn auctioneer."

Les gave Roscoe one of those I-know-just-what-you-mean grins. He ordered another shot for himself and two more beers for us, then he changed the subject.

"How are you boys faring on this circuit, anyway?"

"Not so great," I said. "Me and Roscoe both drawed bad and we're flat broke. But the good news is, we got some good stock drawn this time and we're sure to win something in this show."

"I've been down the road in the same situation you

129

boys are in. It ain't too pretty sometimes, is it?"

Me and Roscoe looked at each other real pathetic like and shook our heads.

Les stuck a toothpick in his mouth and swished it from one corner of his mouth to the other. You could almost see his thoughts flashing across his forehead at the same time. Suddenly he bit down hard and held it in the center of his mouth with his teeth clenched.

"You know, that mean ole woman of mine ain't let me run with any cowboys in five years."

He reached up, took the toothpick out of his mouth, and threw it down on the bar.

"She's gone for the weekend. Ain't no reason you boys couldn't stay at my place until the rodeo is over. What do you say?"

I grinned so big I was afraid I might slobber all over myself.

"Let's find us a sweet thing and have a party," Les hollered. "And, don't forget, boys. The party's on me!"

Free booze and a place to stay. What more could we ask for? There was never a shortage of "buckle bunnies" in Williams during the rodeo. We found one for each of us. In fact, ole Les ended up with two. They said they were from Utah and used to be married to the same man. I don't know if they were putting him on or not, but he sure looked happy.

Les was a pretty darn good storyteller, too. He gathered up four other cowboys and their dates and started telling them all about his mean wife. He was really starting to have fun. Now, cowboys don't need permission to have a good time, but when some poor old boy like Les has five long years to catch up on, well, we just figure it's our civic duty to do everything within our power to see to it he enjoys himself. So, when the bar closed and he invited us to go on up to his house, the whole darn bunch of us went along.

Les lived in a mansion all right. It was the most elegant house I'd ever seen — at least, when we arrived it was. Everybody made themselves at home right off. One of the girls turned on the hi-fi and her boyfriend cranked it up as loud as it'd go. The party was on. They raided the bar, sampling everything in the liquor cabinet. Three couples started dancing, and one old cowboy went to chasing two girls up and down the spiral staircase, whooping and hollering, and generally having a ball. But me and Roscoe had more immediate concerns. We were starved to death.

We headed for the kitchen to find something to eat, and we were in luck. There was a loaf of bread on the counter and plenty of ham and cheese in the fridge, so we started making sandwiches. We were gobbling them down about as fast as we could slap them together. I think we must have ate four or five each. Anyway, I could tell we were hungrier than usual because, for once in our lives, we were thinking ahead. While Roscoe was checking out the rest of the groceries, I spotted a basket of eggs just waiting to be gathered. So, I went and found Les and asked him to come back to the kitchen for a minute.

"Hey Les, does your wife collect eggs or what?"

"That's the same question I asked her. She has this friend that raises chickens for a hobby. Ain't that the damnedest thing you ever heard — raising chickens for a hobby? Anyhow, she keeps giving us all these eggs and I'm allergic to the damn things. So, go ahead. Fry up a dozen. There's some ham in there, too. Eat all you want."

I didn't bother to tell him we'd finished off the ham. I was still thinking ahead. I knew boiled eggs would keep quite awhile and Roscoe and me would have something to take down the road with us.

"Les, do you mind if we boil some up to take with us tomorrow?"

"Take the whole bunch if you want to. I just keep throwing the damn things out, anyway. Go ahead! Help yourself, boys, but right now there's two gals in the other room wanting to tell me all about polygamy."

Les let out a war whoop and headed for the living room, and Roscoe went and grabbed us a bottle of Jack Daniels. He set it on the table by the stove while I looked for a big pot to boil those eggs in. I had planned to talk our dates into doing the cooking for us, but they were both passed out on the rec room floor. Me and Roscoe didn't care, though. Our minds were still on our stomachs, and with that black-labeled bottle of cowboy cooking sherry and music blaring in the background, boiling eggs was not a real big chore.

I filled up the biggest kettle I could find with water and put it on the stove. The eggs were just starting to boil when everything got quiet. That got our attention real quick. We had a couple more shots of whiskey and went to see what had happened.

When I peeked into the other room, I realized the party was over. Les' wife had come home early. She was standing in the doorway, staring directly at her husband who was sprawled out in a big easy chair next to the fireplace. With a beer in one hand, a cigar in the other, and a girl on each knee, he looked rather busy — and real drunk. He had no idea that danger was lurking.

His wife marched towards him, hands on her hips and blood in her eyes, and planted her feet smack-dab in front of that easy-chair. Her voice sent chills down my spine. She sounded just like one of them Marine drill sergeants, and it wouldn't have surprised me a bit if she'd been wearing army boots. I was afraid she'd have the whole bunch of us doing push-ups and scrubbing latrines after she got finished with Les. I was glad she turned on him first. She sounded off.

"What the hell do you think you're doing?"

Les tried to get out of the chair and both girls fell on the floor. Still gripping the beer bottle and cigar, his hands shot up in the air like a cop had just yelled "Hands up!"

"Now, Honey," he slurred. "Who are you gonna believe? Me, or your lying eyes?"

With one slap of her hand, that woman sent both the bottle and cigar sailing across the room. When she picked up the fireplace shovel the girls didn't need any further encouragement. They gathered themselves up off the floor and made a speedy exit just as she hit Les up side the head with the shovel. She swung again, but it was bent from the first blow and she missed. Les ducked anyway, and rolled out onto the floor.

Everybody but me and Roscoe had run for cover, and things looked pretty bad for Les. There he was lying face down on the floor with that wild woman standing over him with a shovel. I thought about trying to disarm her, but . . . well, I consider myself a brave man, but riding a two-thousand-pound bull and disarming a mad wife with a fireplace shovel are two different things. The first requires a little courage and a lot of stupidity. The latter is

133

nothing short of a death wish, and I had no desire to die young. Besides, I was still hungry.

When Les tried to crawl away, she pinned him down with one foot stuck square in the middle of his back.

"You sorry son-of-a-bitch!" she wailed. "I'll make you think, my lying eyes. My ass!"

"Marybeth, you're gonna break my back. Please, let's talk this over before . . ."

Marybeth sure was a sweet-sounding name for such a foul-mouthed old gal. She never let up. She was all over Les like a cheap suit. And the way she was cussing, I expected Roscoe to start blushing any minute.

Suddenly I remembered the eggs.

"Hey, Roscoe," I whispered. "If we're gonna help that ole bull rider, we better think of something quick because that pot's gonna boil dry and ruin our eggs."

Roscoe was doing some real serious thinking when he saw Les stumble to his feet and make a break for the kitchen. Marybeth was right on his heels, and that's when he saw his chance to save the old boy's hide. He jumped into her path and cut her off.

The two of us went flying through the kitchen, nearly knocking Les off his wobbly little bow-legs. We each grabbed a handle on the pot of eggs, but that dang thing was red hot. I didn't see any pot-holders, so I reached for the tablecloth, dragging salt and pepper shakers, a Lazy-Susan full of knickknacks and our cowboy cooking sherry behind us. When I wrapped the tablecloth around the pot, the whole mess crashed to the floor. It was enough to stop Marybeth dead in her tracks again.

Now, carrying a pot of boiling water with five dozen eggs in it is not easy after you've darned near finished off

134

a bottle of whiskey. The water was splashing over the sides, scalding our hands and forearms, and making a slimy mess under our feet. But we were determined to get out of there with those eggs.

With Les leading the way, Roscoe and me headed for the back door, juggling our pot full of precious eggs. There was no way we were going to give up those eggs now, even if it meant getting whopped on the head with a shovel. But Marybeth had traded her shovel for the fireplace broom and, like that pot, she hadn't cooled off one bit. I hollered at Les to open the screendoor, but the dang thing was locked and he fell down trying to unlatch it.

"Look out, boys," he said as he hid behind the two of us like we might have shielded him from that witch and her broom.

Marybeth was a hell of a marksman, too. She managed to beat me and Roscoe severely about the head and shoulders before we could attempt our great escape.

Without a free hand to open the door, I was desperate. I looked at Roscoe and yelled: "On three! One — two — three!"

We charged the door and knocked it clean off its hinges. The three of us barreled out into the backyard, stumbled over a flower bed and fell in a heap of arms, legs, hats and boots. Marybeth came after us like a mad bull out of a chute, and I thought for sure we'd had it. But I guess she didn't see our pot. She tripped and landed on top of us and lost her broom. While she was crawling around on her hands and knees looking for it, I reached for the pot. Believe it or not, there were still quite a few eggs in it.

Fortunately, Roscoe was roosting on Marybeth's broom, and that gave us enough time to make our next move. I pointed to the barn where I had parked my car, and all three of us jumped up and ran at the same time.

"Les," I said, nearly out of breath when we got to the car, "That wife of yours has her heart set on killing you. You're more than welcome to come with us if you want to."

He was panting hard.

"Damn that woman has got a short fuse. Thanks a lot boys. I think I'll just lay low for a couple of days. She'll run out of steam sooner or later." He rubbed his head and grinned. "It sure was fun, though. Thanks!"

I wondered why he would be thanking us at a time like this, especially when we were about to run off and leave him to face that mean old woman. But, I guess a man can learn to put up with a woman who has that much money and doesn't care how you spend it. About that time we heard her coming. And, boy, was she unhappy!

"There's no use hiding out here, you low-life son-of-a-bitch. The longer it takes me to find you, the worse you're going to suffer, so you had better get your scrawny little ass back in that house or else!"

Les reached around the back of his neck and pulled out an egg that had somehow managed to lodge itself in his shirt collar. He tossed it to Roscoe and thanked us again for the party.

"You boys better get on out of here. Looks like the old lady just ain't in a partying mood tonight."

That sounded like pretty good advice to me, so we hopped in the car and took off. But there was only one way out of there, and that meant driving past Marybeth. The way she was waving her arms, for a minute I thought she was sorry to see us leave. That's when I saw she had found her broom. She hit the front fender with that thing and darn near drove a hole through it.

"Damn, Hoss!" Roscoe hollered. "That woman is serious as death about turning out ole Les's lights. I sure am glad she don't have a gun."

"That makes two of us."

Roscoe took his hat off and started punching the inside of it and bending the brim.

"Just look what she went and done to my hat!"

"Stop worrying about your lid. We got more serious problems than that. Where are we gonna sleep tonight?"

"How about we go back there and knock on the front door?"

"Huh? Are you plum out of your skull?"

Roscoe smiled.

"When his wife answers, we'll just say, real polite like: 'Excuse us ma'am, but your husband said we could spend the night here. If you'll just point us to our room, we'll get a little snooze before the rodeo tomorrow.'"

Roscoe sure enough had a helluva sense of humor.

"And don't forget to tell her to be real quiet in the morning," I laughed. "Because you know how we like to sleep in."

"Yea! That otta really turn her pilot light up."

"Tell you what, partner. I'll drive back there, but you have to knock on the door."

Roscoe rubbed the top of his head and put his hat back on.

"Well, maybe next time," he said after he'd thought about it awhile. "I know. Maybe we could get a calf roper to do it. When that gal comes uncorked, I'll bet one of them ole boys would come off that porch faster than he

137

goes down a rope to a calf."

It is a well-known fact that rough-stock riders and the timed-event boys don't get along too good. We never pass up a chance to take a pot shot at one another, and Roscoe and me were always dreaming up ways to get calf ropers in trouble. But the rest of the cowboys had got the hell out of there long before we had escaped, and there was no telling where they were now.

"Well, at least we got away with our groceries," Roscoe said as he pointed to the eggs in the back seat. "But I think we'd better roll all the windows down and drive fast."

"Why's that?"

Back at Les' place, when I peeled out of the driveway trying to dodge the wicked-witch-of-the-west, the pot had tipped over. There was no water left and half the eggs were rolling around on the floorboard.

"You and me are both soaked and that back seat isn't exactly dry. Since it looks like that's where we'll be sleeping tonight . . ."

I stepped on the gas and Roscoe proceeded to roll down the windows.

"Hell, I ain't had to sleep in a wet bed for a long time. Wasn't it last weekend when you got in a chug-a-lug contest with that Okie?"

"Are you saying I wet the bed?" Roscoe sounded a little upset. "I have never wet the bed!"

"All I'm saying is, you didn't leave the toilet seat up."

"Very funny, smart ass. You just do the driving and I'll be the comedian. How's that?"

"Good. I'm sure Bob Hope will sleep better tonight knowing he ain't got any competition."

We made camp at the rodeo grounds that night, and since I was in the driver's seat, I laid claim to the front of the car and made Roscoe sleep in the back. I felt like one of them contortionists, curled around that damn steering wheel like a pretzel, but at least I was dry.

The next morning we decided to go into town and get some coffee. Seeing's how we hadn't had a chance to make any money yet, we figured we could use something hot and wet to wash down those boiled eggs. We asked around and found out there wasn't but one cafe in the whole town, so we crossed the street and headed for the *Sunny Side Up*.

I couldn't believe my eyes when I looked through the window. There was old Les, sitting in the front booth, resting his head in his hands. He was wearing the same clothes he had on the day before and he had a big shiner. We sneaked in the door and slid in the booth with him.

"Holy shit! Just what I need to see the first thing in the morning. Two egg-stealing outlaws. Before you get comfortable, I want your solemn promise. No matter what I say, I don't wan't you helping me have any more fun."

"Wait a minute," I said. "You were the one with a blonde on each knee, smoking that big cigar and sucking on that jug. It ain't our fault you got in trouble. If you'd been smart, you'd sent one of them gals in the kitchen to help us cook. Then you would have only got in half as much trouble."

Les had to laugh.

"You know, boys, I forgot until last night just how much hell cowboys can get into — and how much fun it is. Thanks to you two, it's all coming back to me now."

Roscoe reached over and slapped Les on the back.

139

"That's what friends are for."

"Yea," I agreed. "Hey, Les, it don't look like you got back in the house after we left."

Les got a twinkle in his one good eye.

"No. As a matter of fact, I didn't even try. I walked over to that friend of my wife's — the one that gives her all them damn eggs. I found out something I didn't know before. Her old man is a truck driver and he ain't home much, and turns out she likes cowboys — a lot."

"Uh huh," I said. "Got a new rooster in the coop, does she?"

"Seems like." His smile suddenly turned serious. "I got up early this morning and snuck over to the house to get my car. You know, that looney woman threw all my clothes out in the yard."

"Now, Les, you got to expect . . ." I began.

"Oh, that ain't the bad part."

"What's the bad part?" Roscoe wanted to know.

"The neighbor's got three blue heelers. The whole pack was there tearing my clothes to shreds. And what they didn't tear up, they pissed on."

Me and Roscoe got to laughing so hard, we might near fell out of the booth. But I have to admit, as funny as it seemed, I was starting to feel a little sorry for Les.

"Tell you what, I'll get you some passes for the rodeo. You might as well come with us. You can't get into anymore trouble than you already have."

"I wish I could, boys, but the truck driver will be back in a couple of days, and I gotta make everything up to the little woman."

"Are you sure, Les?"

"It'd be just like the good ole days," Roscoe said.

140

"We could take off down the road, just like you used to."

"It's darn tempting," Les squinted through his black eye. "But, I think I'm a little too old. I can't take a whippin' like I used to."

"Well, partner," I said, "It's been nice knowing you. And we sure do thank you for them eggs. Thank your wife's friend for us, will you?"

"Sure will. And if you boys ever come back to Williams and see an old man with a new Stetson and a brand-new western-cut suit, that'll be me. I've decided my old lady can get away with almost anything, but I'm not gonna give up my duds again."

Les got up, tipped his old hat and waved goodbye. We ordered a couple of coffees-to-go and headed back to the rodeo.

Behind the chutes, the bull riders were rosining up their ropes and checking them for wear. They had plenty of time because the bull riding is always the last event. Roscoe and the rest of the bareback riders already had their gloves on and their riggings out, working the handles over and strapping on their spurs. They were up first. After I put on my leggings, I unstrapped my saddle, sat in it, and dabbed a little saddle soap and rosin on the swells. Then I heated it up by rubbing them on my leggings real fast. (When you get just the right mixture, your legs will stick like glue to the swells of your saddle.)

Roscoe was up first, so I helped him set his rigging during the grand entry. The national anthem was playing when Cotton, the chute boss, yelled:

"Okay, boys. Pull 'em down!"

I stood on the back of the chutes behind Roscoe as he got down on his horse so I could pull him out in case he flipped in the chutes. Roscoe had his hand wedged in tight.

"C'mon, Roscoe," I said. "You got the draw of the herd. Bear down and make a hand."

As soon as the crowd took their seats, Roscoe nodded his head.

"Outside!" he yelled.

They jerked the gate and that horse blew out into the arena, jumping and a-kicking up a storm. Roscoe laid back and was running iron in him. The crowd started cheering. They recognized a good ride when they saw one. When the whistle sounded and he got off on the pick-up man, the clapping, hooting and howling turned to a roar.

"Listen to this, folks," the announcer said. "Seventy-nine for that ride. Give him a big hand."

Roscoe came back to the chutes, grinning from ear to ear.

"That was one hell of a ride!" I told him. "Best I've seen you make in a long time. Looks like you got your lick back."

"It's about time!"

"Way to go, pard. You've done your part. Now it's my turn."

While I was getting ready for the bronc riding, the calf ropers were busy twirling their twine. There's always more calf ropers than ticks on a hound, so I had plenty of time to look over our horses as they were being loaded into the chutes. I drew a big black one called Tar Baby. I'd seen him before and I liked the way he bucked — not too fast, but not so slow you couldn't win money on him.

I haltered and saddled him, and as soon as the last calf had been roped, all the bronc riders pulled their saddles down. My old horse stood real good in the chute, which I was thankful for. Chute fighters can put a world of hurt on a man, and I still hadn't recovered from an incident that happened a few months before. My horse went over backwards in the chute, and I ended up in the El Paso hospital with two cracked vertebrae.

Arizona is just full of team ropers. You can't shake a tree without ten of them falling out of it. And there was about two trees full of those boys in Williams that afternoon. They were up next after us, so they were stacked up in the roping box and all along the fence. They were just sitting there on their horses, jawing, each with a big chew of tobacco stuck in the side of his cheek, spitting and swinging their ropes. It was annoying.

"Roscoe, why in the hell did all of them boys have to come into the arena now? Can't they just wait till after we're finished riding?"

"You don't need to worry about them, Hoss. If one of them gets wiped out, it won't be no big loss."

"Yea, but if they cause one of us bronc riders to get killed . . . well, that would be a tragedy."

"You're a sick man. Now, get on this sucker and win some money."

I measured my rein, pulled my hat down, eased into the saddle, and got my stirrups. I shook my face and Tar Baby turned when they jerked the gate. But he didn't bale out like he usually did. He took a run first, then headed straight for the team ropers who were all wadded up around the roping box. Forty feet away from them he broke and went to bucking. I got in perfect time, dragging hair from his shoulders to the cantle of my saddle with every jump. Just as we reached that pack of fools, the

143

whistle blew and old Tar Baby jumped right into the middle of them. That's when the rodeo really got started.

I'll say one thing. Those boys are damn good at roping, but they ain't worth spit when it comes to riding a bucking horse. None of them was paying attention, so when their horses started bucking and squealing, their hats and ropes went flying every which way. Hollering and cussing, they were hanging on to those saddle horns for all they were worth. I'll bet half of them ended up swallowing their tobacco.

I had blown a stirrup, and I sure didn't want to get bucked off with all those hooves flying. So, as I rode by this one big old fat boy, I leaned forward, grabbed him around the neck and swung off my horse. That fella must have been glued to his saddle horn, and he wasn't real happy about having a passenger.

"Let go, you crazy son-of-a-bitch!"

His horse was on the run, and when I felt him slipping out of the saddle, I hit the ground a-running. That cowboy landed in a cloud of dust so big, even his buddies couldn't see him. They ran right over him, and that's when I made a run for the chutes. I didn't want to be around when those boys got untangled. They all had ropes, and unless I missed my guess, there was a good chance they'd be looking to hang a certain bronc rider I knew.

Everyone behind the chutes was in hysterics, including Cotton.

"Son, you otta be in the circus."

It took awhile for the announcer to give my score. And when he finally got around to it, there was still such a commotion, we could barely hear him.

"That last ride was a sixty-five, folks, but we'll give

him an extra ninety-five for the excitement he caused."

When the show was over, Roscoe ended up winning the bareback riding and I got third in saddle broncs.

"Say, Hoss," he said to me as we gathered up our gear, "We've got enough moola to have a big steak before the dance tonight. What do you say?"

I looked at him like he was nuts.

"For the ass-whipping we took to get those eggs, we ain't about to waste our money on food right now. We'll probably need it farther on down the road. You know how a cowboy's luck is. We might not hit another lick for a spell."

"You might be right at that, Hoss. No sense in wasting good groceries."

For the next two days we ate nothing but eggs, which we washed down with a whole bunch of cold beer. We went on down the road, our pockets jingling, and hoping our luck would hold out until the next show.

Now, Roscoe was a good old boy. The kind I could have gone down the road with the rest of the season. But several days of beer and eggs put one helluva strain on our relationship, if you know what I mean. Don't get me wrong . . . I'm grateful we had them. Still, to this day, I haven't been able to eat another boiled egg.

KAMIKAZE COURT

I've heard it said that everybody has his day in court, even cowboys. And I suppose I've had more than my share of days in court. But the one I remember most was in Pecos, Texas where old Roy Bean sat as judge and jury. (Not on my case, of course.) They say he was sure enough an ornery old cuss, but if I had to live in Pecos, I'd be real hard to get along with, too. That place might as well be in another galaxy. There's just miles and miles of nothing but miles and miles. It's so hot and dry, even the jack rabbits carry canteens. According to legend, Judge Roy Bean was a harsh man in his sentencing, too. Still, I'm relatively certain that I would rather have faced old Bean himself than Kamikaze. But I'm getting ahead of myself.

One warm summer afternoon, after drinking a few cold beers, a buddy of mine named Monty talked me into going to the Pecos rodeo. Pecos' claim-to-fame is that it was the site of the first rodeo ever held in the United States. Now, that's probably true, because as far I could tell, that's all that Pecos would ever have to brag about.

"It's an easy show," Monty said. "None of the toughs make it because it's too far out of the way."

That part was sure enough right. A person had to get lost to end up in Pecos. You damn sure wouldn't go there because you wanted to. Anyhow, the rodeo part sounded good to me, so we pulled out for Pecos and the Fourth of July rodeo.

146

Monty should have mentioned how damned hot it was, too. But . . . well, live and learn, I guess. We drove into town with our cowboy air-conditioning on full blast — doing sixty with all the windows rolled down — and skidded right up to the front door of the rodeo office. That didn't impress the sweet thing behind the counter a whole lot, so we paid our entry fees real quick like and got back in the pickup. I put my foot to the floor and we peeled out of there almost as fast as we had drove in.

Since I had never rode stock in Pecos before, I drove on out to the rodeo grounds to take a look at what they had. The bulls were damn sure big and strong. Even Monty seemed a little surprised. The one I had drawed was just sort of wandering around the pen, hooking the hell out of anything that got near him. He looked mean enough to put a hole in any cowboy stupid enough to give him a chance. So, when he headed towards me, I backed away, and when I looked up I saw two buzzards circling over me. That made me so nervous I went to shuffling my feet. Well, Monty thought that was funny as hell. He had a weird sense of humor. Monty rode barebacks, and he was convinced that bull riders were not wrapped too tight. But then, everybody thought that about us, and come to think of it, they were probably right.

"What's the matter, Hoss? Them buzzards got you scared?"

"It's a bad omen, Monty. You know it is."

Most cowboys are a little superstitious, and a bad omen like that would be hard for any bull rider to ignore.

"Aw heck! They're just trying to intimidate you."

"And they're doing a damn good job of it, too. I don't like the way this thing is starting out already.

147

Looks like I got the meanest, hookingest bull in the whole herd, and these bone-pickers know it. They're just hanging around waiting for the kill."

Monty, being the good buddy that he was, just had to reassure me that everything was normal.

"Well, Hoss, they got to eat, too, you know."

He slapped me on the back and hee-hawed like that was the biggest joke of the century. That's when I got to discussing his ancestral heritage.

"I'm gonna keep the keys to the pickup hid so if I get killed, you'll have to walk across that blazing desert to get home. Then those birds can have you for dessert."

"Oh quit complaining. You've lived a whole lot longer than me or anyone else ever thought you would. Every morning you wake up again is a surprise, and you know it."

"That may be true, but . . . Damn! Who wants to die in Pecos, Texas? None of my girlfriends would even be able to find this place. They would cry over me if I didn't come home."

"Cry over you?" Monty laughed. "They'd probably fight the buzzards to see who could pick at you first."

"Would not!"

"Would too. What about that brunette gal from Albuquerque — the one you dated while you was going out with her sister — *and* her momma?"

"Okay . . . maybe one of them wouldn't mind so much if I was deceased, but . . ."

"One of them, hell! Remember the redhead from Deadwood who caught you in the back seat of her Corvette with her Mexican maid. I'll bet she'd like to tear off a piece of your hide. And the little blonde in Lubbock that you lost in a poker game. Oh yeah, and the one . . ."

"I get your point." I interrupted because I knew he wasn't going to shut up unless I did. "But I think you ought to know, there's one gal in Portales that would wear black for a year if something happened to me."

"Oh sure, Hoss. But your momma don't count."

I was about to take offense to his last remark when the rodeo clown drove up. I closed my eyes and crossed my fingers, hoping it was Wick Peth. Wick was the best rodeo clown that ever lived. If he couldn't keep a man-eating bull off of you, no one could. There wasn't a bull rider going down the road that old Wick hadn't saved at least once, and he had saved my life at least twice.

When the door opened, I seen it was old Juice. He leaned out and waved to Monty. Now, Juice was no slouch, either. There was a lot of cowboys had Juice to thank for getting them out of some darn tight spots. Besides, Juice was a good ole boy and he sure knew how to party.

"Hey boys, come over here and help me some, would you? I'm pretty crippled up and I need somebody to help me get ready for the show."

He crawled out of his car and my heart stopped. His left knee was so swollen he could hardly walk. Monty and me scooted over there real quick.

"Juice, what happened to you?"

"Oh hell, I got freight-trained by a bull down in San Antonio two weeks ago. Tore this sucker up real good and I can't hardly put any weight on it."

I might have had a fighting chance if it had been Wick in the car, but fate was not kind to me that day. Oh well, I really knew it couldn't have been him. He was bound to be at one of the big shows on the Fourth of July. He probably wouldn't have given Pecos a second thought. But it would sure have been a comfort to see him.

I bent over to get a closer look at Juice's leg.

"You ain't gonna work this show with a wheel like that are you? Even I wouldn't do that!"

"I told them people I was in bad shape and couldn't even save my own life, let alone anyone else. But they said with all the rodeos going on this weekend there wasn't another clown to be had anywhere."

"They don't have to have a clown," Monty said. "Do they?"

"Sure do! That's the rules. You got to have a clown or you can't have a rodeo. That's how come I showed up — so they wouldn't have to cancel the show."

This whole trip was going down hill fast. I was about to face the meanest bull in Pecos, and those idiots had hired a one-legged clown to protect me. Things were going from bad to worse. I swallowed hard.

"Juice, do you know this ole bull, Kamikaze?"

Juice screwed up is face like he was in terrible pain.

"Hoss, if that's what you drawed, you're in a world of hurt. That ole bull sure is rank. Course, you can win on him. It's after the tooter that he's so bad. Can't get away from him. He'll camp on you and you can't pull him off. He's just like ole Judge Bean. He'll hang your butt."

Oh boy! A bad hooking bull, buzzards circling overhead, a crippled clown, and a buddy who can't wait for me to die so he and the rest of the world can have a big party. Nobody can have that much bad luck in one day.

The bull riding didn't usually get started until about ten. I had resigned myself to the fact that the odds were

150

pretty good I was going to get killed, and I got to thinking about what I had done all my life. There had been a few close calls, I had to admit. It had been fun, but I sure did hate for it to end in Pecos.

The show started right on time that night. Monty was up in the bareback competiton, but him and all those other idiots in that event were giving us bull riders hell. They had heard about Juice and they knew this was a bad pen of bulls. Might near every one of them looked like he couldn't wait to hook your clothes off and blow snot in your face. They were the kind that would eat you plum alive. Some contractors will pick a string like that on purpose — especially if they have been bull riders them-selves. I don't know why, except maybe riding bulls makes you sadistic.

"Say, boys," one of Monty's buddies hollered at us. "Don't you all wish you were just bareback riders now? Then you wouldn't have to ride them mean ole bulls."

Cowboys always poked fun at one another, but I was really not in the mood. I let them have it.

"Who'd want to go through life with one arm three inches longer than the other from hanging on to an ole snatching horse? You can't even buy a shirt that fits right."

One of the younger boys held out his arms and measured his sleeves.

"You're full of shit!" he yelled back at me.

"I am not! I'll bet not a one of you can see if your boots are on the right feet. You've had your heads snapped back so much you can't look no way but up. And you've all had your tail bones broke so many times you can't sit down. I'd just hate to have to spend the rest of my life standing 'cause my butt hurt."

151

"It beats getting killed," Monty said.

Damn, I hated it when he was right. I was thankful Monty nodded to let his horse out. I had a feeling I was going to lose the debate.

Monty's horse didn't buck too good, but he rode him. And since they were getting two head in all the events, he was still in the average. When he got back to the chutes he was ready for a drink.

"Hoss! Give me your keys and I'll go get us a jug. I'll be back in time to pull your rope. I wouldn't miss that for the world. Besides, someone has to give you last rites."

Then he laughed. The sick moron!

I wasn't the only shifty-eyed bull rider there. A few of the other boys had rode this stock before, and they were saying how hard it was to stay alive, even with healthy clowns. According to them, every bull in the pen was a head-hunter. But Kamikaze was the worst.

"He'll enjoy having you for lunch," said one old veteran who knew what he was talking about and had the scars to prove it.

That didn't make me feel any better.

It's hell being the last event in the rodeo sometimes. While the rest of the show was going on, the bull riders were pacing back and forth, mumbling to themselves and generally acting pretty darn nervous. Any other time I would have raised a little hell until it was time to get in the chute. But I figured I needed all my strength that night — just in case I had to raise myself from the dead.

Finally they started loading the bulls — big old racks and all. They had one helluva time driving them down the chutes with those horns sticking into everything that moved, and anything that didn't move fast enough.

When the slide gates closed, that's when those suckers really came uncorked. They kicked, hooked and bawled, and even tried to climb over the top of the chutes. It was real clear they had a terrible disliking for bucking chutes and anything associated with them.

Kamikaze was the fourth one in, and what he was doing to that chute would have made Jesse James' blood run cold. He got upside down, sideways and standing on his head. A shiver ran down my spine. I figured if he broke both my legs before he got out of the chute, at least I wouldn't have to go out there and get the rest of my body torn to pieces.

I slipped my rope on him and he just exploded. So did the rest of the bulls. The chutes were all popping, cracking and swaying. At this rate, I thought maybe they would tear the whole place apart — escape, leave town, hell, leave the country! But no such luck. Those chutes held like the defenders of the Alamo.

About then Monty showed up, sucking on a jug with that stupid grin pasted on his face.

"Damn! I could hear them loading these things clear in town."

"You know, I believe you are telling me the truth for once. These old fellas are plum loco!"

"I told that guy at the package store they just had a bunch of milk pen calves in the bull riding this year. He sure laughed."

I knew, right then and there, if I lived through this ride I was going to kill me one smart ass bareback rider.

Monty was waiting for me to reply to his little joke when Juice hobbled over to the chutes.

"Boys, you had better hit the ground running because I can't help you. You're on your own. Every man for himself."

He could have saved his breath. All of us had done figured that out early.

The first guy out rode about five jumps before he turned back to the left and got bucked off. He landed on his hands and knees and started scooting as fast as he could for the fence, but the bull was hard after him. He was only halfway up the fence when that sucker stuck a horn in him and flipped him ten feet over to the other side. He hit the ground like a rock. It hurt me just to watch him get up, but he didn't seem to be injured too bad.

After just three jumps, the next rider got thrown clear back into the chute. He was almost over the back side when his bull decided to climb in behind him and bury his rack in the cowboy's butt. That poor fella blasted off like a rocket ship. He flew over the side and took out two other boys standing behind the chute, too. They all landed in a big pile, cussing to beat the dickens, and the bull just stood there like he was king of the hill.

"Damn, Monty! Did you see that? That damn bull climbed a fence to get to that ole boy. What in the hell do they feed these sons-of-bitches, anyway?"

Monty never even tried to change the expression on his face.

"Raw meat and gun powder."

That was it! I was definitely going to kill him now.

The boy in front of me was next. When he slid down on his bull I almost apologized to Monty for lying to me. I'll say one thing for that kid — he put a hell of a ride on that bull in the chute. His might near got his knee caps hammered to a pulp. Finally he got his rope pulled. He scooted up, shook his face, and the bull blew out of there like a bullet, hit two jumps and cracked it back to the right, threw his head up and jerked that cowboy down at the same time, catching him right between the eyes with a horn. It knocked him smooth out and he flipped over right in the bull's face. His hand was still hung in the rope. That didn't really improve the bull's disposition any. In fact, he took a dim view of some smelly cowboy dangling in front of him. He started banging the boy's head between his horns like a ping pong ball. And when he got tired of that little game, he shook him every which way until his hand came out of the rope. Then he threw him like a rag doll, twenty feet straight up in the air, stomped around in a circle till he hit the ground, and ran over him. I guess he just wanted to make sure he was dead.

The crowd was on its feet at first, but the cheering had died down by the time the pick-up man rode up. He hit the bull in the face with his rope just enough to distract him while a couple of other cowboys dragged the kid out of the arena. Two ambulance attendants loaded him onto a stretcher and headed out.

Three outs and three hookings. So far, the bulls were way ahead. I stood on the chutes looking down at old Kamikaze — the worst one of the bunch. I got a real uneasy feeling in the pit of my stomach, wondering what a man was supposed to say before he dies.

Monty was still his usual cheerful self.

"Tell me again what it is you like about bull riding, Hoss. Don't you just envy us bareback riders?" he grinned. "Get off on a pick-up horse, never have to run for our lives from a mad bull. Ain't never too beat up to enjoy the party after the show."

This guy was really getting on my nerves. If he didn't shut his yap soon, he was going to be too dead to think about a party.

The time of reckoning had arrived. I was up. I slid down on Kamikaze and right off he went to banging around and blowing hard.

"Just listen to that," Monty said. "He's sucking in a lot of air because he knows he'll need it to catch you and blow out your pilot light."

I should have hit him right then, but all I wanted to do at that moment was get out on this chute-fighting son-of-a-bitch. That bull was about to break my legs off at the knees. I shook my face, they opened the latch and Kamikaze blew out of the gate. He hit three jumps, cracked it back to the left, spun around, then jumped out of the spin and went right. He might near jerked me down on his head, but I got back up just as his horn zipped by my nose. About four more wraps and the whistle blew, but he wasn't letting me off that easy. He went to spinning again and, as soon as I started to reach for my wrap, he jumped out and threw me off the right side into my hand. I was hung up in my rope.

Being hung up scares the hell out of all bull riders, and after watching the kid that was up ahead of me, I wasn't afraid to admit to myself that I was scared. Hell, that bull was dancing around in a circle, spinning left, twirling to the right, wacking me in the head with those horns, and my feet weren't even touching the ground. But I must have had enough adrenaline in me to fill a ten-gallon can. Suddenly everything seemed to be happening in slow motion. I grabbed a hold of the tail of my rope and pulled. Just as my hand came loose he stepped on my foot, spun around again, hit me in the butt, rolled me up in a ball and ran over me. I saw one of my boots go sailing in the other direction and I remember thinking, this shit is getting old!

Kamikaze must have been thinking the same thing. He stood still for a second or two, dropped his head, shook the snot off his face, glared at me with those mean ole black eyes and hooked his right horn under my back. He flipped me over like a pancake, ran the length of me again and again, flipped me a couple more times, and if that wasn't enough he ran up behind me and stepped square in my face, braking a couple of ribs at the same time. Whether he was wore out or going back to find him another cowboy to kill, I don't know, but he trotted off to the catching pens like it was just another day at the ranch.

I couldn't move. I had so many knots on my head, even my hair hurt. I could hear the crowd cheering and feet thumping towards me. It was Juice hopping across the arena to help me. He patted me on the shoulder and that damn near finished me off.

"You sure know how to thrill the crowd, Hoss."

I knew right then him and Monty must be kin — both smart asses. I got up and staggered towards the chutes. Blood was running everywhere and I could hardly breathe. I found my boot, and Juice picked up my hat, which wasn't really worth his effort.

I sure was busted up. My bottom lip was split clear down to my chin and my nose was squashed flat. The only part of my shirt that wasn't ruined was the collar and the cuffs. I put my boot back on and stumbled over behind the chute where Monty was standing.

"Damn, Hoss, you sure are good watching. I ain't

had this much fun since the pigs ate my little brother."

Even in my condition I was looking for something to hit him with. I went to cussing and that's when I realized my front teeth were all knocked loose.

"Are you hurt?" he asked, lifting up what was left of my shirt to have a look at my ribs. "I'd say it looks like you tripped and fell down. And just let me say something about your appearance. You really need to clean up more often. Your clothes are a disgrace. You know, Hoss, if you want to be seen with me, you're just gonna have to spend more time on your personal hygiene."

I was too sore to spit or I would have.

There's only one thing worse than being mangled by a bull, and that's being too banged up to make it to the dance. I might have looked like I was dead, but I had no intention of missing that dance. I found a piece of tape and pulled my lip together. Juice had an extra bandage, so I took off what was left of my shirt, soaked it in a stock tank and wiped off all the blood. Juice helped tape my ribs up. Then I borrowed a couple of pencils and worked them up each nostril to reshape my nose. Lucky, there was a clean shirt in my war bag.

"Give me that jug!" I said to Monty. I won the first go and I ain't dead yet. Probably I'll wish I was tomorrow morning, but right now I feel like dancing."

I took a big pull on the jug. With all the open cuts on my face, I figured I needed a good dose of disinfectant. It hurt a little going down, and my eyes watered some, but after the third of fourth swallow, my aches and pains started to ease up.

When a nice guy like me meets up with a bad ole bull like Kamikaze, chances are the bull won't remember too much about it. And, after a month or so, a cowboy has a way of getting over the pain and suffering of a ride such as the one I had that night. But I doubt I shall ever forget or forgive my buddies for the abuse I suffered after the rodeo. What they done was just plain criminal. They laughed and made fun of me so bad, if I had killed the whole dang bunch of them, even Judge Bean would have let me off. But, being the nice guy that I am, I kept my mouth shut — except to take a drink — and waited for my run of bad luck to end. I knew I had a reprieve coming soon.

Monty offered to drive us to the dance. I swear he did that just so he could hit all the pot holes. The bumping and bouncing made my ribs hurt even more, but I kept nursing that bottle, and by the time we got to the dance I was better. I eased out of the pickup and walked real slow over to the hall. Monty found a table near the door. I was in no condition to defend myself and I would need to make a quick exit if a fight broke out. I sat down, carefully, and we ordered drinks. Before the waitress got back, a couple of blondes started our way.

It's true what they say about good things coming in two's. The girls were twins — tall, long-legged and just about as pretty as any rodeo queens I'd ever seen.

"Weren't you boys in the rodeo?"

"Yea," Monty stood up. "I'm one of those handsome bronc riders, and this fella here is one of them idiot bull riders."

I was just about to smack him when both girls spoke up at once.

"Ooh, we like bull riders."

"Well then," I said with a smile as wide as the Rio Grande, "Tonight is your lucky night."

159

Each of them pulled up a chair beside me.

"My name is Jill and this is my sister, Jan."

Jan looked down at the floor and smiled.

"Jan's shy," Jill continued. "Most people call us the Lovett girls."

"We're twins," the shy one spoke up.

I snickered at old Monty who looked kinda lonely sitting there all by himself in the corner.

"Isn't it dangerous riding those nasty old bulls?" Jill asked me.

"What?" Monty interrupted. "You all are crazy! Everybody knows bull riders are nothing but a bunch of show-offs."

The girls took offense to his remark.

"Who's your rude friend?" Jill asked.

"Oh him. He's not really my friend. Just a guy I picked up hitchhiking on the way to the rodeo."

Well, that really ticked old Monty off.

"I'm leaving!"

Of course, he didn't. He sat right where he was.

"That bull got you good, didn't he?" Jan said.

Jill pulled up a little closer to take a look at my wounds, and before I knew it the two of them were oohing and awing, kissing my "owies" and petting me like a dog.

"We felt so sorry for that poor cowboy they took to the hospital," said Jan.

"Yea," Jill smiled sympathetically. "We were afraid you might have to go, too."

"Me, too. I'm a little bent, but it ain't nothing that a pair of fair-haired ladies couldn't cure."

Jan got a proud look on her face as if she had just discovered the theory of relativity or something.

160

"Well, there are two of us."

"Yea!" I grinned. "There is at that!"

"Oh, tell us all about your ride," Jill squealed. "Please."

So, I did.

Pretty soon they were fighting over who was going to buy me the next drink. They wanted to hear more stories and, as usual, I was happy to oblige. Monty kept trying to horn in, but the girls ignored him like he wasn't even there. In fact, we were all wishing he would just go away. Finally he got fed up.

"This place is a bore! Let's get out of here."

The girls pleaded: "Oh no! Don't go, Dan."

They positioned themselves around me like they were circling the wagons to ward off an Indian attack.

"I'm leaving, Hoss. If you don't come now, you'll have to find your own way."

"We'll take you," Jill said to me.

I looked over at Monty and shrugged.

"Daddy just bought us a speedy little convertible." Jan smiled. "Where do you want to go?"

"Well, I . . . I reckon I'll go back to the hotel after the dance," I said.

That's all Monty could take. He jumped out of his chair and slammed it up against the table.

"Now, don't you just wish you were a bull rider, Monty?" I yelled as he stomped out the door. "I never seen no bareback rider sail off into the sunset in a new sports car with the Lovett girls before. Have you?"

For two hours those girls listened while I entertained them with my wild west stories. When the band started playing, everyone else got up to dance, but the

161

sisters didn't seem to care that I couldn't. They bought all the drinks, too, and I just know that bartender told everybody in the place. I guess I was probably the envy of every cowboy in Pecos that night.

When Monty came back and offered me one last chance for a ride, I turned him down. The Lovett twins had done made me a far better proposition. Those girls had more curves than Wolf Creek Pass and, like a pair of salt-and-pepper shakers, they never went anywhere alone. Only a fool would say no to a pair like that, and I was no fool. Well, at least not in this situation. They took me home and played Florence Nightingale in tandem, and by early the next morning I was feeling like brand-new.

Now, I am not a vindictive man. So, even though I knew that Monty had slept all night outside the dance hall, I saw no reason to rub it in.

"Morning, Monty," I said real civil like. "How'd you sleep last night?"

That's all. I didn't say another word.

Monty didn't speak to me all day. That in itself almost made my encounter with Kamikaze worth it. I got to thinking — I survived one of the wildest bull rides I'd ever had, the Lovett girls had started me a fan club, and Monty was so p.o.'d he couldn't even cuss at me. Life was pretty good.

But, there was something important I wanted to do before I left Pecos that day. I had to get back to the rodeo grounds. Lucky for me, one of the stock contractors recognized my battle scars and stopped to talk to me, so I hitched a ride with him. When I walked over to the pens, there was Kamikaze in the corner, shaking his head like he had a hangover. The contractor was feeding the other stock, so I went and got an extra flake off his stack of hay and threw it to the old bull. He buried his nose in it, and when he came up for air, I think I saw him wink at me.

THE WEDDING

It has been said that cowboys have an unusual sense of humor. I don't know exactly what they mean by unusual, but no one has ever accused me of having a lack of one. A sense of humor has a way of getting a man into trouble, though. And I have to admit, cowboys always manage to find plenty of that. In fact, trouble and bad luck run together sometimes. It generally happens when a momentous occasion is about to occur — like a wedding, for instance. Weddings make cowboys nervous. And a nervous cowboy is liable to make a mockery of any sacred event, even though all he really wants to do is liven things up a bit. Hell, we like to have fun, and inappropriate as it might be at times, a good laugh is a sure cure for nervousness. Of course, add a little bug juice, and nervous or not, we will find a way of taking any special event and ruining the entire affair.

I had been home for a change, when my good good buddy Jake called me and insisted I meet him down at the local watering hole because he had an announcement to make.

"Hoss," he said, "I'm going to marry Shirley."

"Well, I'll be . . . Shirley is a good ole gal, Jake."

"Uh-huh. And since you're the best friend I've got, I want you to be my best man, you lucky devil."

I had to think about it a minute. I guess I should have felt honored, but the truth is, anytime anyone mentions marriage to me, I kinda go into shock. Then I started remembering all the things a best man gets to do and I began to feel a whole lot better about accepting the job.

"Sure thing, Jake. I'll not only be your best man, I'm gonna make your last days as a bachelor ones you'll never forget."

Jake knew what was about to take place. We had rodeoed and partied together for years. All the cowboys we knew liked to have a good time, but the two of us were considered infamous when it came to partying. To us, a good party was almost excuse enough to get married in the first place.

We had about two or three wild days ahead of us but we were ready. Anyone wanting to go down the road with us had better have his hat pulled down, because it was going to be horse shit and gunsmoke. Most guys couldn't stand to make over two runs in a row with Jake and me. Their hearts just couldn't take it, and their wives and girlfriends wouldn't tolerate it. I guess we were a little on the wild side, but there's nothing much to do in the eastern part of New Mexico except raise hell. Besides, it's a hundred miles between anywhere and there's sure nothing to look at.

Jake took me by Shirley's place first. I was worried how she would take the news. Shirley liked me well enough, but she knew that the two of us were trouble when we got together.

"Hi, Honey," Jake said when we walked in. "Dan here said he'd be my best man."

"Correction, partner. I already am the best man. But Shirley met you first."

A little flattery can go along way, I thought.

165

"Uh-huh. With a lead like that, I know you two are up to no good."

Jake walked over and put his arms around her.

"Honey, you've never been suspicious before."

"Yea?" she smiled. "Well you two bring out the best in me."

One of the things I liked best about Shirley was her sense of humor. And she'd be needing it with old Jake.

"Jake," I said, "The first thing we got to do is make a run to Juarez."

"Wait one minute!" Shirley's smile had disappeared. "Why do you have to go to Mexico?"

"You don't think we could get away with having Jake's bachelor party on American soil, do you?"

"Yea!" Jake chimed in.

"And just what do you plan to do down there that you can't do here?"

If I had told her, she probably would have made Jake elope with her that night, spoiling all their wedding plans. I sure didn't want to have to take the blame for messing up that fancy wedding. I had to come up with a convincing answer real quick like.

"We're just gonna have a party — a few drinks and some laughs. You wouldn't deny a dying man — I mean a man dying to get married — one last party. Would you?"

"Very funny, Dan. Now, somebody, answer my question before I get mad."

"You tell her, Jake," I said, trying to buy some time to think of something better.

"No, you go ahead."

"No, no. I insist. You tell her."

Shirley was getting impatient.

166

"Stop arguing and tell me now, or else!"

"Okay," I said. "I wanted to save this as a surprise, but now I guess I have to tell you."

"So . . . tell me!"

"I know how much money you've spent on this big wedding already, and I know how hard it is, financially, for newlyweds, and . . ."

"Really, Dan? Now, how would you know about all that stuff?"

"Well, I hear things," I stammered, "And I read. I saw one of them *New Bride* magazines at the store just the other day. Made me think about you, Shirley."

I thought Jake was going to crack up, and then all three of us started laughing.

"I'm serious," I said. "Shirley, you two will have a whole lot more money to set up house if we do our partying in Mexico."

"Why is that?"

"Because tequila is a nickel a shot. Hell, we pay a quarter for beer down at the bar. Just think of all the money we'll save."

"Yea," Jake grinned. "Just think of it!"

"Is that the best you two can do?"

"On short notice," I smiled real big, "That's the best I can do."

"Well, I know tequila is cheap, but I also know that means you bums will drink twice as much of it — for twice as long — and you won't save a dime because a dime will buy you two more shots!"

"But, Honey," Jake protested. "You gotta have more faith in me that that."

"Aw, come on, Shirley. If we stay around here, you

167

know we're gonna get in some kind of trouble. We always do. You wouldn't want to have to bail ole Jake out of jail on your wedding day, would you?"

"Now, that I'll buy. When it comes to a couple of outlaws like you two, I'm sure the Mexican police will gladly escort you back to the border."

She stared at us for a moment, probably wondering if she should ask more questions.

"Okay, okay, go! I don't want to know what you're doing, but you had better be back in a week. That's plenty of time to act like a bunch of idiots. I want this thing to come off nice and smooth, so don't screw it up. The dress rehearsal is on Friday. Be there!"

"Now Honey, don't worry. We're just going to have a little party. We'll be right back, and then you can tell us what to do. We'll sure enough see that it gets done up right. Won't we, Hoss?"

"Yes ma'am! In fact, you'll be able to tell ole Jake here what to do for the rest of his life. He's been saying how much he's looking forward to it."

Shirley lightened up a little, even though she knew that was a lie, because neither one of us had ever followed instructions of any kind. We'd never done anything anyone had ever told us to do in our lives, and we sure hadn't done anything up right, let alone for a wedding. Our minds were made up and there would be no talking us out of it. She gritted her teeth and reminded us once more.

"A week from today, seven o'clock, at the church. There's only one church in town, so don't come telling me you couldn't find it, either."

In unison, Jake and me promised her: "Don't you worry none. You can count on us."

Shirley laughed, wondering no doubt, if she would ever see either of us again.

"Jake, I got an idea. Let's swing by and pick up Buzz and Delbert. They've never been to Mexico before, and Delbert said they wanted to go with us the next time we went."

I had met Buzz and Delbert at college. Delbert was trying to learn how to ride broncs and Buzz was his roommate. They lived in a little house off campus. Buzz didn't want to rodeo any, but he liked cowboys and always wanted to hang out with us. I'm not sure why. He was kind of quiet, especially after he got to drinking.

We pulled up in front of the house, Jake leaned on the horn, and I ran up to the door. When I told those boys where we were going, they might near knocked me down getting to the car.

It was over three hundred miles to Juarez, and only three towns of any size along the way. But there were lots of honky tonks, and we tried our level best not to miss a one. After all, this was Jake's last days of freedom and we wanted him to have a real good time. It took a dozen bars, six or seven fights, five cases of beer, enough whiskey to fill a bathtub, and two full days to get to the border. We were already about broke, so we couldn't wait to get to sunny Juarez where tequila was three-fifty a gallon and a glass a beer cost only a dime. We left the car on the north bank of the Rio Grande and stumbled across the bridge.

"What is that smell?" Delbert asked.

I grinned.

"That, my boy, is Mexico. Sweet, ain't it?"

"No! It stinks like a barnyard!"

"You'll get used to it," Jake said. "What do you

think about it, Buzz?"

Buzz's head spun around like a top. I had already figured out from that blank stare on his face that he couldn't hold his liquor. After just a few belts, his brain went on tilt like a pinball machine. I had a sneaking suspicion he didn't even know he had left the house. The good part was, he wasn't any trouble. He just kept mumbling and humming to himself, and we led him around like a little dog on a string. Had to keep him away from fire hydrants, though.

I didn't want to walk around Juarez at night. Experience teaches you a lot, and I had known a couple of cowboys who disappeared without a trace. Besides, we had promised Shirley we'd be back.

"C'mon, you all, let's get a taxi. I know where there's a bar across town with cheap tequila. We can start there and work our way back."

It's never a problem getting a taxi in Juarez. The drivers get kick-backs from the local bars, so they darn near run you over trying to get your business. Since I knew exactly where we were going, I asked the first cabbie that drove up how much it'd cost to take us to the *Cup of Gold*. He didn't even try to talk us into going somewhere else. Only locals and frequent visitors knew that bar. It was a little hole-in-the-wall joint with cheap booze.

"One dollar," he grinned. "For all of you!"

Jake had Buzz by the collar so he wouldn't wander off. We put him in the back with us and I told Delbert to get in the front with the driver. I did that on purpose. On the way down, he had bugged the hell out of me about my driving. This was my chance to get even.

That driver took off like I expected him to — foot to

the floor, wide open, eyes forward and straight through the intersection, barely missing a group of tourists who were trying to cross the street. I swear there were sixty potholes in every block, and that guy must have hit every one of them, deliberately. Of course, at fifty miles an hour, it was hard to miss. That old Chevy didn't have any shocks left, either. It just bounced from pothole to pothole, and every so often it would hit the curb. But the cabbie knew the road well. He would just straighten her out and floored it again.

Delbert was having a fit. His face turned white.

"Watch out for that car!" he screamed. "Oh shit! You just missed that guy! Slow this damn thing down!"

Me and Jake thought it was a hoot. We knew how these cabbies drove. In fact, anytime we needed to sober up in Juarez, we just took a taxi ride. It was a sure-fire way to get your heart pumping.

The driver was enjoying our little joke, too. The more Delbert complained the wilder he got. Grinning from ear to ear, he turned around and started jabbering away to me and Jake as the Chevy slid around a corner and headed up a narrow alley. None of the streets was wide enough for two cars. When we met an oncoming vehicle, we both had to run up on the sidewalk to avoid a head-on.

Delbert finally lost it.

"Stop! Let me out!"

The driver tried to explain that it was still two more miles to the *Cup of Gold*.

"I don't care. You're crazy! You're going to get us all killed."

Delbert had a hold of the door handle like he was welded to it. I'm sure he would have jumped if we had slowed down, but the cabbie never got below thirty. Delbert was so scared he started yelling to pedestrians as we whizzed by.

"Help me!" he hollered to a woman who had a bunch of little barefoot kids hanging on to her skirts. "Call the police. They're holding me hostage."

We barely missed running over their toes when we hit the curb. But the locals were used to it. Me and Jake made silly faces and pointed our fingers at Delbert. They just figured he was another gringo acting like an idiot. The kids waved and giggled, which didn't improve Delbert's disposition any. Out of desperation, he put his hands over his eyes and crawled down on the floorboard. He looked like he was praying.

When the cabbie pulled up in front of the *Cup of Gold* he was laughing as hard as Jake and me. I gave him an extra dollar and he helped me pull Delbert out of the car before he peeled off to get his next customers.

Delbert's knees were so weak he could hardly stand up. He was still white as a sheet.

"I think I peed my britches," he whimpered.

"Don't worry about it," I tried to reassure him. "Everyone does that on their first taxi ride in Juarez."

"I need a drink," he said. "That ride just ruined a twenty-dollar drunk."

"You're in luck, pard. At five cents a shot, a dollar can sure get you on the road to recovery."

Jake had quite a time dragging Buzz out of the back seat. When he got him pried loose, Buzz headed for the curio shop next door to the bar. He had spied a little confederate flag in the window and that started him to humming *Dixie*. As Jake watched him staggering around

172

like a zombie, I was sure he was wondering how in the world, out of all of our friends, I had talked him into bringing these two.

"This is a helluva crew we got," he said to me. "One is a damn space cadet and the other isn't potty-trained yet."

"Yea," I grinned. "We do know how to pick 'em, don't we, pard?"

We all ordered tequila. I think Buzz passed out before his drink came, but I'm not sure. I don't remember anything else until the next morning. At that time in Juarez the bars would let you sleep in the booths, which is exactly where Jake and me woke up.

Buzz and Delbert had already been next door to the curio shop, and the first thing I saw when I opened my eyes was two Mexican sombreros. With their serapes and spurs, they looked like a couple of real banditos, and I think Jake believed they were, for a minute.

"Uh, I don't have any money," he mumbled, rubbing his eyes and pointing at me. "That guy over there has it all."

For the next two days we worked our way across town, trying not to miss a bar. On the third day Jake told me we had better start heading back, and Buzz and Delbert were all for that.

"Don't you two ever eat?" asked Delbert.

"Not if we can help it," Jake said. "Food costs money and we need all our money for booze."

"I sure don't want any more to drink," Buzz said. "I've got a helluva hangover. My stomach's rumbling so loud, it's making my head ache."

"Well, I know just the thing to perk you up."

173

Jake went and bought two gallons of jalapenos, and I sprung for a couple of gallons of tequila — one for him and one for me for the ride home. And, since Jake was afraid he might never see Juarez again, he bought three more gallons.

When we got back to the car, we told Delbert and Buzz to get in the back, and Jake handed one of the jars of jalapenos to Buzz.

"Now, all you need to do is eat as many of these things as you can. Then Dan will let you have some of his tequila to wash them down. The peppers cause some kind of chemical reaction that prevents hangovers."

Both of them looked suspicious.

"Are you sure about that?" Delbert asked.

"Of course I'm sure! That's what the Mexicans do. Ain't that right, Hoss?"

"Yes sir," I said as I swallowed one of the peppers. "You never seen a drunk Mexican have you?"

Buzz turned to Delbert and shrugged.

"We've been so drunk since we left, I ain't even sure I've seen any Mexicans."

"Well, look at ole Dan there," Jake said. "He's already finished off half a gallon of peppers. He don't have a hangover and he ain't drunk."

The part about the peppers was true. There was never a pepper on God's green earth too hot for me. Most of them weren't hot enough.

Buzz leaned over the front seat to check out the jar.

"Goddman, look at that. He ain't lying, Delbert."

I started swallowing those peppers like they was popcorn and those two fools stared at me like I had a rare, incurable disease. Meanwhile, Jake kept pouring on the bullshit.

"Don't be too impressed, now," he said. "You all know ole Dan's mother was one of them fire-eaters in the circus before she met his paw, didn't you?

"Oh yea," Delbert gave Buzz a dumb look. "I think I heard that somewhere."

I was trying real hard not to laugh, so I was glad when the boys finally lost interest in me and decided to sample their peppers. But it wasn't any time at all before Delbert let out a scream.

"Holy shit! I can't eat these damn things. My mouth is on fire."

I handed him my bottle of tequila. He took a swig but he was still smoking. Buzz didn't seem to be having any problems, though. He tipped up my jug and started guzzling like it was water.

"Hey!" I yelled. "Don't you know you can go blind if you drink too much of that stuff?"

"Yea, that's right," Jake said. "It happened to a buddy of ours. He looked just fine all night while we were partying. But the next morning he was blind as a bat. Never saw the light of day again."

Buzz looked at Delbert who was starting to get a little panicky.

"Don't we have anything else to eat besides jalapenos?" he asked.

When I told him no, he stared at the jar for a minute, then set his jaw.

"Well, I don't care. I'll take my chances. I ain't gonna eat any more of those barbecue coals."

"Suit yourself," Jake said.

The next morning when me and Jake woke up, we had no idea where we were. The four of us were sprawled out in a meadow somewhere in the mountains. The car was there, but no road — anywhere.

"Jake, when in the hell did you drive us out here?"

"I wasn't driving."

"Then who was?"

"Hell if I know."

I peered over at the two banditos who were out cold, their serapes over their heads.

"Must have been them," I said.

Jake took a look and shook his head.

"No way."

Ten minutes later we still hadn't figured it out, and we were starting to argue about which way we were going to leave, when two Indians walked up from out of nowhere. They looked like they had just been to a pow-wow with their old horse blankets wrapped around them. One had a purple band tied around his head, and neither of them was wearing shoes.

I guess they must have been surprised to find two cowboys and two wild-looking bandito types lying around in a pasture with a couple of gallon jugs between them. They started chattering away to each other, and that woke Delbert up. He poked his head out from under his serape, sat up on an old log, then lost his balance. He was shaking so bad he had to straddle it and hold on with both hands to keep from sliding off. About that time, Buzz started moving. He stumbled around humming *Dixie* until he found a tree to lean against, and then proceeded to relieve himself. I really don't think he had woken up yet.

"Look like you had big party," the Indian with the headband said as he walked towards us.

I figured this was no time to act unfriendly, even if

I was still upset with Jake for bringing us to this God-forsaken place.

"Get down here, Chief, and have a drink. This man here," I said, pointing to Jake, "Has done lost his mind. He's getting married, so we're giving him a big send off. You want to help?"

The last word wasn't out of my mouth before he had flopped down beside us and was reaching for the tequila. His partner didn't need an invitation. He came a-single-footing it as fast as he could, heading right for Delbert's log.

"Help! run for your life," Delbert screamed "We're being attacked by Indians."

At first I thought he was putting on an act, but that meal of peppers and tequila must have really fried his brain. He tripped over the log and fell on his head, driving his sombrero over his eyes so he couldn't see. Then he really went to screaming.

"I'm blind. Oh, my God! I'm blind."

I guess he did believe Jake after all. With his head still on the ground and his butt in the air, he went to turning circles. His feet were going around clockwise, chewing up the ground like a rotor tiller that's gone hay-wire. When that serape got wrapped around his neck so tight he couldn't breathe, he collapsed in a heap.

The Chief was having the time of his life, sipping and a-chuckling with a big gleam in his eye.

"I get like dat when I drink too many," he grinned, and then he let out a little war whoop, just for the fun of it.

That started Jake off, and me and the Chief's partner joined in. Delbert was sure the whole tribe was after him. He tried to run, but his legs got tangled in his serape

177

and he fell over, knocking his sombrero off. He was sure surprised he could see again. But Jake wasn't about to let the show end there.

"Hey, Delbert. See this man here?" He pointed to the Chief. "He's going to scalp you."

Delbert rolled back on his heels, his eyes bugged out, he took one look at the Chief and passed out.

While all this was going on, Buzz hadn't moved. He was propped up against his tree, a glazed look in his eyes, and as far as anyone could tell, he hadn't missed a bar of *Dixie.* I was going to offer him a drink, but I figured the Chief's partner ought to have his share.

That old boy's eyes lit up and I thought he was going to suck the bottom out of the bottle. He finally put it down, wiped his mouth, stuck out his hand and introduced himself to me and Jake.

"Hi! I'm Joe. Me and Charley were just wandering around with a big hangover wishing we had a drink when we saw you. What are doing here?"

"That's a damn good question. Where is here, anyway?" I asked, pointing my finger into the dirt.

"This is the Mescalero Indian Reservation," Joe said real proud like. "How did you get here? The nearest road is two miles away."

"I have no idea," I said. "Better ask Jake here. He's the driver."

"I wasn't driving. I was too drunk. You were the one behind the wheel the last time I looked."

"Then you must have been telling me where to go, because I . . ."

"Lucky we found you," Charley interrupted. "How much tequila you got left?"

178

"I ain't too sure," Jake scratched the back of his head. "Several gallons, I think."

Charley and Joe grinned. While they were muttering away at each other, trying to figure out how we had got our car up the side of the mountain without hitting any trees or falling into a canyon, I went and grabbed another jug out of the trunk. I knew right then and there we were not going to get out of there without having a party, so I started thinking ahead. There were just two things on my mind at that point: what day was it, and which direction was home.

"Say, Charley," I said as I offered him another drink, "Do you have any idea what day is today?"

"Nope."

"Joe?"

"Who cares?"

I looked at Jake and he looked back at me like it was my fault we had lost track of the time.

"Hell, I don't know, but we had better find out soon. If I don't show up for that practice wedding, Shirley will kill us both."

After a few more pulls on the jug, Joe decided that it must be Tuesday, and Charley reminded us that we should start celebrating Jake's bachelor party before it got too late.

"We give you big Indian send off," he said with a grin so big I thought is old teeth would fall out.

The Indians didn't lie — about the party, that is. The next day when we woke up about noon with the sun shining in our bloodshot eyes, they were gone, and so was our tequila.

Lucky for us, I had asked them how to get off the

reservation before I got completely tanked. We poured Buzz and Delbert back into the car and took off to look for the gas station Joe had told us about. We found it easy enough, and they had gas, too. They also knew what day it was. Rehearsal day!

With nearly three hundred miles to go and less than six hours to get there, I let the hammer down. That speedometer needle was looking at numbers it had never seen before, which caused Delbert to start whining about my driving.

"When are you going to land this thing?" he said right before he turned pale and passed out again.

We didn't stop until we got to the church. It was exactly five minutes to seven when we came sliding up in a cloud of dust and gravel. Jake slapped Delbert awake while I went and picked Buzz up out of the dirt. He'd fallen out of car. None of us was walking too straight, but we managed to stumble up the church stairs — except for Delbert. He couldn't quite make it, so he crawled the rest of the way on his hands and knees. Jake kicked the door open with the heel of his boot.

"We made it, Honey," he yelled. "Just like I said we would."

Jake and me staggered down the aisle to where Shirley and her folks were standing with the preacher. Buzz followed along like a faithful dog and leaned up against the pew behind us. He was a sight! He smelled, too, and his zipper was open. He didn't have a clue where he was, and he kept facing the back of the church. When he did turn around, those two red coals he had for eyes made him look like a mad bandito. Meanwhile, Delbert had crawled up on one of the pews and was snoring to beat sixty.

180

The preacher stood there with his mouth open when he saw me and Jake. I guess we didn't look too good, either. None of us had taken a bath in a week. Our clothes were filthy, we hadn't shaved, and we must have reeked of booze. I tried to straighten myself up a little — tucked my shirt tail in and dusted my boots off on the back of my pant legs. Jake did the same. That didn't impress Shirley any. She was furious!

Jake took it like a real gentleman, teetering a little, but smiling politely with that faraway look in his eye. Shirley chewed on him for all he was worth, and when she ran out of words — clean ones, that is — Jake looked her straight in the eye and said:

"I'm sorry, Honey. Were you saying something?"

It was a good thing we were in a church. That was the only thing that stopped Shirley from killing him. Her mother just shook her head, recalling her own experiences with Shirley's dad, no doubt. He had been a rounder in his younger days, and I had heard he'd taken part in a few bachelor parties himself. He thought the whole thing was pretty hilarious.

When Shirley got her breath back, she jumped on me.

"You're supposed to be his best friend. Why didn't you take care of him? Don't you want us to get married? How could you?"

"I got him here on time. That's all you asked me to do. What did you expect? A couple of choir boys?"

"Choir boys! You two are about as close to choir boys as Satan's hounds!"

When the preacher cleared his throat, Shirley shut up, but only for a minute.

181

"You're right, Dan," she mumbled through her clenched teeth. "I ought to know better than expect anything else out of you two. You did get here on the right day — that's a first!"

With Delbert's snoring echoing in the rafters, and Buzz wandering around asking everyone where he was, it's a miracle that preacher didn't cancel the whole affair. Jake and me managed to stumble through it without upsetting Shirley any more than she already was. But, after it was over, we realized she hadn't fully regained her sense of humor.

"This is it, you two!" she said, cornering us on the steps outside. "Get your butts home and sleep it off. And for God's sake take a bath. You stink! You had better be on time tomorrow night or you'll be wishing someone was changing *your* names!"

We promised we would be there at seven and made a fast exit. We drove back to Buzz and Delbert's house, and all four of us stumbled inside and crashed. When Delbert woke up, he found out just what kind of chemical reaction you get from jalapenos and tequila. He screamed every time he went near the bathroom. After listening to that for an hour or more, me and Jake couldn't take anymore, so we went outside to clean up the car.

Now, we meant to do exactly what Shirley had told us to. We really did. We would have, too, except Jake found part of a gallon of tequila in the trunk. Well, it just seemed like a waste to throw it away, so we each took a little sip. The next thing we knew, we barely had time to get dressed for the wedding.

"Oh shit!" Jake hollered when he looked at the clock. "Hoss, we got to get ready fast."

I had borrowed a suit from my cousin which I had wadded up in a ball and stuffed in the trunk before we took off for Mexico. When I put it on, Jake might near had a fit.

"Hoss, you can't go looking like that! Hell, you gotta do something with that suit."

I hunted around and found an iron and ironing board, and Jake helped me set it up. I had never ironed in my life, but I had seen it done, and I knew I had to learn how real fast. I had no other choice. Since we were in a hurry, I turned the iron on high. Now, if I had really known anything about ironing, I would have known that was the wrong setting for this kind of material. I discovered that after putting three or four little holes in the pants. My vision wasn't what I wished it was, and I probably wouldn't have noticed if Jake hadn't pointed them out to me. Then I grabbed my tie, which was nylon, and hit that with the iron. To my surprise, the end of it shriveled up like a little wad of used tin foil. But it was too late to do anything about it. I owned one tie, and that was it. So, I just fixed it as best I could. Jake and the boys were already in the car waiting on me.

It was about twenty minutes past seven when we screeched into the church parking lot. We ran for the back door and found the preacher pacing up and down. He got one whiff of us and covered his face with his sleeve.

"Lord help us. I've got a mad woman out there and you two . . . if you cause another disturbance . . . there's innocent bystanders . . ."

Jake slapped the preacher on the back.

"You worry too much, pard. Me and ole Dan here stay in worse trouble than this most of the time. Just

183

remember one thing. If you hear a hammer cock, duck!"

The preacher's face turned gray.

"Thank you, that's very comforting."

"Hey, Dan," Delbert whispered. "What am I supposed to do?"

Delbert had volunteered to be part of the wedding party, but I had forgotten that he was asleep during the rehearsal. Hell, he'd never even been to a wedding before. My eyes lit up.

"You see those four candles over there by the altar? When they start playing the Wedding March, you go over and blow them out, one by one. When you're done, one of the bridesmaids will blow out the candles on the other side."

"Is that all?"

"Yep. That's it."

"Now, don't get in a hurry," Jake joined in. "Do it slow and solemn like."

"Okay, Jake."

We walked in and took our places. Jake stood next to the preacher, grinning at Shirley who was on her Dad's arm at the other end of the church. She was glaring at all of us. I looked down and that's when I saw the curly end of my tie sticking out. I tucked it into my shirt real quick and then the music began. Shirley and her Dad started making their way down the aisle. When they were about halfway, I punched Delbert in the ribs.

"Now!" I whispered loud enough that one old gal in the third row gave me a dirty look.

Delbert stepped real slow over to the first candle, leaned back, puffed his cheeks out and blew hard. I thought the curtain behind the altar was going to burst into flame.

The preacher glanced over at me and made a nervous-sounding noise in his throat, and the bridesmaid's mouth dropped open like someone had hit her in the head with a two-by-four.

Except for a couple of little gasps and some faint whispering, the rest of the congregation remained quiet. But, by the time Delbert got to the second candle, Shirley's Dad had figured out what was going on. First his lips trembled, then he started snickering. And when he just could not hold it back any longer, he bust out laughing. Shirley had a hold of his coat sleeve and was trying to drag him down the aisle, but he was laughing so hard he couldn't get his feet to move.

Delbert was about to extinguish the third flame when the place erupted in laughter. He turned around to see what all the commotion was about, and that's when he realized he had just pulled the biggest boner of all time. One look at the woman in the white veil and he knew he was a dead man. He ran for that back door and he was gone faster than that preacher could blink.

Me and Jake were laughing so hard, we had to hold each other up, and even Shirley's sense of humor finally caught up with her. In fact, I think the only serious one left in the church was Buzz. He didn't know where he was but he was his usual congenial self.

"Bartender," he belched, "Next round is on me."

After awhile we pulled ourselves together and went on with the ceremony. One of the ushers had to shush Buzz up when he went to humming *Dixie* again, but other than that we finished the wedding without a hitch. The reception was another thing, altogether.

Two glasses of champagne was all Jake needed to

get himself pickled again. He hit Shirley in the nose with the slice of wedding cake he was trying to feed to her, and then he took her garter off, pulled back on it like it was a slingshot, and let her rip. It hit the preacher smack-dab in the eye.

Meanwhile, I was outside preparing the wedding coach. That was one job I knew I could handle. I wanted to fix it up cowboy style. Three or four tin cans and an old shoe on a string wouldn't do justice to a cowboy wedding. I used barbed wire. First I attached a big metal trashcan to the bumper, then I tied on an empty gasoline can, an old washtub and a half-a-dozen quart-size juice cans. When Shirley and Jake took out of the parking lot, the noise was deafening.

Most guys would have stopped and cut all that mess loose. Not Jake. He had it in his mind to outrun us and get rid of the junk later — somewhere we couldn't find him. So, he tore through town with that mobile salvage yard dragging behind him, making more racket than a Fourth of July parade. Every time that old car turned a corner, its tail would scoot over to the other lane, causing oncoming traffic to zig-zig all over the place. A couple of pedestrians had to jump out of the way real quick, too. Those beat-up juice cans were flying in all directions, and they were lethal.

When the horn-tooting procession reached the outskirts of town, it was time to give up. Jake had led many a chase trying to outrun the local do-right boys, and he knew every backroad in the next three counties. He would have got everybody lost — everybody but me, that is. I was usually the one driving on them other runs.

I guess Jake figured I would give up, too, because

186

he was awful darn determined to get rid of me. He drug that junk for five miles or more. Finally the clatter must have got on Shirley's nerves — or maybe it just jarred loose some of the dust in that old pickled head of Jake's. I'm not sure which it was, but when he figured out I wasn't going to let him out of my sight, he pulled over onto the shoulder and stopped.

"Hey, pard," I yelled. "I got some wire cutters I'm willing to sell real cheap."

That barbed wire had coiled itself around the bumper like a snake. I think Jake was glad I had followed him after all. We had one helluva time untangling that mess.

After cussing a little and laughing a whole bunch, we said our good-byes. Jake hopped back in his car, I waved to Shirley, and the newlyweds sped off for their honeymoon — safe at last.

Believe it or not, Shirley eventually forgave me. In fact, they named their first-born son after me. Buzz went to work for the Border Patrol, and Joe and Charley started a pack guide outfit. As for Delbert . . . well, if you see him, just don't mention the wedding.

187

A COWBOY IN YANKEE LAND

I always liked to rodeo back east. The shows weren't too tough and you got on a lot of stock — at least five head in every event — and if you made the whistle, you usually won some money. The rodeo in Chicago was a ten-day show, so a guy could do pretty darn good if he put his mind to it. But, cowboys have a way of getting bored real easy — even in a town as big as Chicago. After a day or two, we usually start to looking for unique ways to entertain ourselves.

During the sixties, most of the rodeo cowboys that I knew lived in the Southwest, and any place that a cowboy didn't live was considered Yankee Land. Now, the people who lived in Yankee Land weren't used to being around a bunch of oversized boys in big hats that chew tobacco, drink with both hands, tell wild stories, and just generally raise hell. Believe it or not, when we went to towns like New York or Milwaukee, we met a lot of dudes who thought we were still fighting off the Indians in Arizona, or that Mexican bandits slipped across the Rio Grande on dark nights to kidnap pretty women. Hell, some of them silly girls we met thought we did nothing but sit around campfires playing guitars and singing cowboy songs. Probably believed that we rode into town every night to see Miss Kitty, too.

Now, I already had me a reputation for being rather windy. In fact, I had been accused a time or two of being windy enough to turn every windmill in Texas. But those folks back east made a storyteller's job easy. I swear, they would believe almost anything I told them. I always made my tales sound true, though, no matter how farfetched they really were. And I guess they appreciated them because they always made sure my glass was full. Yarn-spinning is real thirsty work and I was grateful, too. Of course, the more I drank, the wilder the stories got.

Back in those days, I think a lot of people figured anyone who wore boots and a hat was about as honest as old Ben Cartwright himself. Those Hollywood cowboys made storytelling a cinch. If my tale started out a little slim, I'd just fill in the details with a few scenes from *Rawhide* or *Bonanza*. They hardly ever questioned me, and if I happened to see someone with a suspicious look, I'd just give my best John Wayne stare, lower my voice and talk real serious like.

"You ever known a cowboy to tell anything but the God's honest truth?" I would ask innocently.

They would admit they hadn't, of course, because the only cowboys they had ever seen were Gary Cooper at the movies or Matt Dillon on *Gunsmoke*. And everybody knew those fellas were straight as a string. Besides, my stories were entertaining.

Anyhow, I was looking forward to the show in Chicago, even though it was a ten-day affair. Trouble is, I didn't have a whole lot of money, and my old pickup definitely would not get that far without a few minor repairs. The brakes were shot, it had no second gear, and worse than that, the heater didn't work. It was around Thanksgiving, and everyone else I knew was either broke like me, or didn't want to go way up north at that time of year. My options were limited.

I had a colt that was really put together and showed some smarts, and I knew a rancher that was also a calf

189

roper. He had told me that his old roping horse was starting to show his age, and he thought my colt might make a good replacement in two or three years. He had wanted to buy it, but I had put him off. Now that colt was my ace in the hole.

I called the roper.

"Hi Blink. You know that colt you've had your eye on? If you'll come over right now, he's yours."

"Hoss, that sounds mighty good to me. I'll be there in thirty minutes."

I wasn't too sure how he was going to do that, because he lived almost sixty miles down the road. But after I thought about it for a minute, it didn't sound all that impossible — for Blink, that is.

Several years back, when we were both amateurs, we had made a few rodeos together. He always drove like he was the pilot of a spaceship — real heavy on the throttle and easy on the brake. He thought the brake pedal was a nuisance. In fact, I don't remember if he ever used it. I always felt sorry for his horses, too. They would break out in a sweat just thinking about riding in that trailer when he was driving. That rig wouldn't touch down but every twenty feet. If you looked back through the window to the trailer, you could see those poor critters with their front legs up in the hay manger, hiding their eyes so they wouldn't have to watch.

Already I was starting to feel guilty about selling that colt, but I knew Blink would be halfway down the road by now and it was too late to change my mind.

Now, that old roper could be anywhere in the blink of an eye, and you might think that's how he got his name. But that wasn't the reason. He was called Blink because he didn't. He squinted a whole lot, but I never saw him blink. I always got a little nervous if I had to look at him too long because it reminded me of staring at a snake. He had a big head like an Appaloosa horse. His face was red as a baby's butt and those two squinty eyes of his were smack-dab in the center of it. Blink was not a pretty man.

Sure enough, thirty minutes later his old car and trailer came skidding in the drive, hitting every high spot at least twice. He headed it uphill to the barn, and when it rolled to a stop, he hopped out.

"Hoss," he squinted at me, "I don't know what changed your mind, but I'm sure glad you did. That colt will make me a good roping horse someday."

I wasn't really all that fond of twine twirlers in general, but I liked Blink. He was a sure-enough cowboy and the best match roper I'd ever seen. In a ten-calf roping, he couldn't be beaten. He had ice water for blood. Nothing rattled him, and he never made a mistake.

"Tell me," he said. "What made you decide to sell this little fella?"

"I'm just restless. I want to get away to a rodeo, so I thought I'd make the Chicago show."

"Going to give those Yankees hell are you, Hoss? Not a bad idea. What poor fool are you going with?"

"I guess I'll have to go by myself. I can't find anyone to go with me."

"That sure don't surprise me none. Every dang cowboy around here knows there's trouble just about every place you go."

He was right about that. Any cowboy in his right mind, or his left mind — or for that matter, any guy with half a mind — wouldn't want to go with me unless he was desperate, or stupid.

"How's your old truck running?"

"My old truck ain't going to make it this time. I guess I'll take the train. It don't cost much more than the bus, and I just hate buses. I called while I was waiting for you to get here. They said there was a train leaving at midnight. Would you mind running me up to the station so I can leave my truck here."

"Sure, Hoss. I'll just drop the trailer here and get it and the colt on the way back."

I was ready to go. Blink helped me load my things into the car and we drove to town. With Blink driving, we were there plenty early. In fact, I had over an hour to kill. With the cash he gave me for the colt, I ran into the train station and bought my ticket, then we headed across the street to the bar for a little toddy.

When we walked in, I heard a familiar voice.

"Hey, Hoss, Blink. Over here!"

It was an old buddy of ours from Clovis, and he was sitting with some cowboys that I'd run with. Pretty soon we got to reminiscing about our escapades and that's when Blink brought up the subject of Chicago.

"Why in the hell are you going way up there in the dead of winter?" asked one old cowboy.

"Well, I gotta find some fresh meat somewhere. You all won't believe a damn thing I say anymore, and besides, those poor people have to find out about cowboys and the wild west some way. My version is a whole lot more interesting than what's in them history books."

They all nodded in agreement with that, except one clown who was shaking his head like he was real sad to see me leave.

192

"Well, there's one town that'll never be the same."

The next morning when I woke up on the train, I went to the dining car and had some breakfast — to kill time until the club car opened. When it did finally open, I was the first customer. But it started to fill up after awhile, and as soon as those wild-eyed passengers saw my hat, they all wanted to know if I was a real cowboy. A good-looking Stetson rarely gets ignored.

"You bet, I am," I said proudly. "I am a real, honest-to-goodness cowboy from the land of enchantment — New Mexico."

A group from California, headed home to Chicago for the holidays, gathered around and started buying me drinks. They asked all sorts of dumb questions like "Where's your lasso?" and "Don't it hurt them poor little cows when a full-grown man like you rides them?" They didn't even know there was a rodeo in Chicago, so I wasn't surprised when one guy asked if New Mexico was still as wild as it is on TV.

I pulled my hat down a little closer to my eyes and pretended I was Gary Cooper.

"Pretty much. The big towns are about half civilized, but out in the country where I live there's still lots of outlaws, Indians and rustlers and such."

Now, that was a stretch of the truth, but just a little. After all, there was an old Indian man and his wife that lived on the east side of town. As for the rustlers, well I'm sure there was an occasional brand that got altered. And I was often referred to as an outlaw.

I continued: "In fact, I almost missed this train. My stagecoach broke down and I had to ride one of the horses to get to the station on time."

"Really?" chirped a skinny guy who adjusted his horn-rim glasses like it might help him hear better.

"Really. I rode a big bay gelding."

I couldn't believe they bought that one, but when they did I knew I'd died and gone to heaven. After that it was easy. The stories just came out all by their selves.

While I told them about chasing Indians, capturing cattle rustlers and horse thieves, and gun battles and hangings, they kept buying the drinks. That helped to make the stories more credible, especially if they drank as much tequila as I did. In fact, after I told them that tequila was the official cowboy drink for New Mexico, they all started drinking it. But after a half hour or so it was apparent that tequila was not the official drink of Illinois or California, because they were passing out right and left — or, if they could make it that far, they headed for the marble altar in the bathroom. But for every one I lost, another one showed up. Pretty soon I'd just be telling the same stories all over again. (When I'm on a roll, I don't like to mess with a sure thing.)

By the time we got to Chicago, the whole train was full of drunks, including myself. A few of them had to be carried off the train, but I managed to find my saddle and suitcase and stumbled off the train when it pulled up to the station. With the rest of the drunks slapping me on the back and slurring how good it was to finally meet a real live cowboy, I felt like I was some kind of celebrity. This sure beat sitting at home watching the sand blow, I thought.

I asked the first person I saw how far it was to the nearest hotel. I was hoping it was close because, in my condition, I wasn't sure how far I could get. The guy I asked was new in town, too, but the cop across the street

194

came right over. He must have seen I needed help.

"There's a hotel about three blocks that way. You can't miss it. It takes up most of the block."

He looked me over real good and shook his head. I pulled my hat down low, threw my saddle over my shoulder, picked up my suitcase, and staggered off in the direction he had pointed to.

Train stations and bus stations are generally not located in the finer part of town. Chicago was no different. The people hanging out on the street corners and in the alleys looked pretty pathetic. With all the empty liquor bottles littering the gutters I would probably have fit right in, except for one thing — the outfit. It was clear that a whole lot of people in Chicago had never seen a man wear a cowboy hat. And I know none of them had seen a bronc saddle before. I thought their heads would spin clean off when I walked by.

Suddenly brakes were squealing and I smelled rubber burning. In the middle of the intersection, a young man in a business suit had his arm out the car window, pointing at me and hollering.

"Hey, look at that! A real live cowboy!"

I suppose I shouldn't have been surprised. After all, I was in Yankee Land and everybody around was city folk. I was the only one carrying a saddle. The rest of them had briefcases and umbrellas, or shopping bags from them fancy department stores. I guess I did look a little different. But I didn't expect to damn near cause a wreck.

Thank God the hotel was right where the cop said it was. I entered through the main door, thinking the registration desk would be right inside, but the smoke was thick as fog and I didn't see it right off. I took a few more steps, and when my eyes got used to the haze, I saw a couple dozen winos laid out on old couches. All of them were watching one little twelve-inch, black-and-white TV. I thought to myself, that cop must have figured I was in a whole lot worse shape than I thought I was.

The bums all looked at me like I was a fat and juicy Thanksgiving turkey fresh out of the oven. At that point I didn't even know if I'd make it to the front desk before I got mugged, but they stayed glued to their seats. I figured they were too lazy to get up, or more likely, they just didn't know where to hock a saddle.

When I walked up to the desk, the clerk woke up from his nap. I figured this old boy must be filling in while the regular guy was in the bathroom or something. He sure enough was a mess. The stains on his tee-shirt were a menu of everything he'd eaten for a week, and his eyes were redder than Blink's old bloodhound's. His beard looked like he had started to shave about three days ago, then went and forgot to finish the job.

I thought about shopping for another hotel but a couple of things stopped me. I knew this place would be cowboy cheap, number one. Number two: I was scared I wouldn't make it to another hotel. I knew I probably stood a better chance with a bunch of winos than I did with anybody else I might find on the streets of Chicago at that hour. So, I told the clerk I wanted a room.

He looked up with those droopy eyes and a cigarette hanging out of the side of his mouth, and muttered:

"That'll be a dollar and a quarter."

I was certain that price didn't include room service, so I didn't even ask. When I handed him the cash, he gave me a key, which kind of surprised me since he didn't even bother to ask for my name. I picked up my gear and he pointed across the desk to a pair of swinging doors.

What I found behind those doors could have come directly from the set of a Vincent Price movie. The "hotel," which had been a warehouse at one time, now was one large room, divided into a bunch of little cubicles by unfinished sheets of half-inch plywood. All the cubicles had doors, a colorful assortment that were obviously factory rejects.

My key fit the door with the number assigned to me, but I was sure it probably fit all the others, too. Inside, the "room" was just big enough to accommodate the army cot in the center, and above, nailed to the plywood walls, was a makeshift ceiling of chicken wire. At that point I figured for sure I'd wake up the next day and see hens laying their eggs up there.

Now, I am not a fussy man, and I like to rough it as much as the next cowboy, but I had my doubts as to whether Fort Apache was going to stand up to an assault by the Wino Commandos if they decided to storm the place. For a brief moment, I think I knew how Custer must have felt, knowing he was outnumbered a hundred to one. I swallowed hard and decided, if I survived the night, this would at least be a good story for the trip home. I slid one end of the cot snug against the door and threw my saddle on the other end for a pillow. Too tired to worry anymore, I laid down and passed out.

The next morning I woke up — a surprise in itself — and headed out as fast as I could. With all that gear to pack, and not knowing exactly where I was going, I decided to take a cab to the stock yards. That was the second surprise. The rodeo was held in the coliseum there, and the cabbie knew exactly how to get there. He also knew all about rodeos. It sure was nice to finally meet someone I could talk to for a change. I found out later that he had a brother-in-law who was a bareback rider.

While I was at the office paying my entry fees, I ran into a bunch of my buddies. With a few more familiar faces around, Chicago was beginning to feel a little more friendly, and I couldn't wait to tell them about my midnight adventure.

"It was a whole lot of fun riding the train with that bunch of Yankees," I told them, "But if I do it again, I think I'll stay away from the hotels near the depot."

When I went to describing the flophouse where I had spent the night, they all had a big laugh — especially Tom, a bow-legged bull rider from Tulsa. Tom was about as tall as a Shetland and just about as pretty.

"Hoss, if you haven't got a place to stay, you can bunk with us."

"Thanks, Tom. Judging by what I seen so far, I guess us cowboys better stick together in this here town."

"Yea," Tom said. "There's only seven or eight in our room. I'm sure we can find a hole for you somewhere. Right, boys?"

The rest of them agreed. After all, eight to a room wasn't all that unusual.

"That'll be good enough for me. Just something to keep the cold off."

I could hardly believe my eyes when we walked up to the Southside Hotel. Compared to the dump down by the depot, this place was a palace. I guess it had cost them plenty, but those old boys were making sure they got their money's worth. That room was plum full of war bags, saddles, suitcases, boots, hats, whiskey bottles and smoke. A poker game was already in progress, and two dudes were in the bathroom — one in the shower and the other busy shaving about three days growth off his face. I made my way over to the window to get some air, and accidently kicked over one of three cowboy spittoons — actually three empty oil cans.

"All the comforts of home," I said as I found an empty spot in a corner and threw my gear on the floor.

I had met all the guys before except one bronc rider from South Dakota named Lester. I introduced myself.

"Lester, you had better stay away from that guy," Tom warned. "He'll get you in trouble for sure."

"Don't pay any attention to ole Tom here," I grinned. "I only have two bad habits — singing too loud in church and staying too late at the library."

All Tom could do was roll his eyes. He'd known me quite awhile. Lester, on the other hand, seemed to approve of my sense of humor. I knew I right off that me and him were going to get along just fine.

There were two bars and several beer stands at the coliseum, so nobody felt they were going to die of thirst. That was a good sign. And, the first three days of the rodeo were good to all of us. That was also a good sign. But after three days we were beginning to get a little bored — which is always a bad sign.

One afternoon between shows, me and some of the boys were killing time out by the stock yards when we came across a team of horses and a wagon. They were just standing there. The wagon was full of hay, so I figured they must have been using it to feed in, because there wasn't anyone else around.

199

"Say boys," I said, "Let's take a little ride."

They didn't need any persuading. We all piled on, I took the reins and away we went. We stopped at one cowboy's pickup for a couple jugs of whiskey and started back towards the coliseum. Those jugs made several fast trips around the wagon, so by the time we reached the coliseum, we were feeling no pain. While I drove up and down the aisles where the show cattle were, the rest of the boys were whooping and hollering, and generally raising hell. They spied some gals over by one of the beer stands and managed to get a couple of them to join us. They must have been half-plastered, too, because they were just as rowdy as we were.

For some reason, rodeo cowboys and whiskey always spells trouble. I'll admit we were drunk and a little loud, but we were just having fun. That's all. And it would have stayed that way if it hadn't been for a bull-dogger named Scooter.

As we were rumbling down one of the aisles, we came across a kid with his show steer. I guess the bull-dogger decided he needed a little practice, so he baled off the wagon and landed right on top of that steer. The boy stood there with his mouth hanging open, holding his lead rope while Scooter tried for all he was worth to lay that steer down. He tugged at its ears, its tail, and just about anything else he could get a hold of. But the kid recovered quickly. He grabbed a broom and started beating the hell out of that knot-head. I figured he might take after us next, so I turned the wagon around and we headed down the next aisle. About that time Tom hollered that he was about to finish off the whiskey.

"Hoss, you'd better find a saloon fast before we run out of fuel."

I popped the reins and the horses took off in a little trot. We were headed in the general direction of the rodeo when I spotted one of the bars. One look and I was convinced they had built it specially for that wagon. It had big wide doors like a barn, and it looked like a perfect fit, so I drove the team in as far as I could and stopped.

When those cowboys fell off the wagon and stumbled up to the bar, the bartenders were dumbfounded. They just stood there like stone statues. I climbed down, cocked my hat, and strolled up behind my buddies.

"Beer for the horses and whiskey for the men."

(I had always wanted to say that.)

We had only been there a minute when here come the do-right boys with ten or twelve people in tow, all yelling and pointing at us like we were sideshow freaks.

"That's them, officers. They're the ones."

When that big old cop with the crooked teeth asked one of the bartenders what was going on, I figured I had better think of something quick.

"Officer, that team ran away and this brave man here," I slapped Lester on the back, "risked life and limb to stop them before somebody got killed."

Lester was weaving back and forth with a sheepish grin on his face. I was kind of hoping he wouldn't open his mouth, because there was no telling what might come out.

"Uh-huh," the cop grunted, drumming his fingers on his belt and looking us over one by one as if we were in a police line-up.

I was grateful when Tom stepped forward to verify my story, but just when I thought we might have them convinced Lester really was a hero, someone in the crowd recognized me.

201

"He's the one that was driving, sir."

I did my best to look innocent.

"Who me?"

The cop called his sidekick over and whispered something in his ear. Then he turned to me.

"All right, Slim. Hands behind your back. You and the hero there are going to jail."

Then the deputy walked over to get Tom. They'd decided to take him, too, I guess because he was handy. This situation did not look good at all. The girls had already vacated the premises and the rest of them drunken cowboys had propped themselves up against the wagon to keep from falling on the floor. I sure didn't like the idea of spending the rest of the rodeo in the cooler, but there was too many to whip and nowhere to run.

"Tom's right about one thing," Lester sputtered as they slipped the handcuffs around his wrists, "It ain't dull being around you."

If I didn't know any better, I would have guessed that ride to the police station was Chicago's grand tour. And believe it or not, I was praying they'd hurry up and get us to that jail, because all that beer and whiskey I had consumed was looking for a place to escape.

As it turned out, we got there just in time. The desk sergeant was about to get off his shift and he was in a good mood. A big man with a barrel chest, red nose and red hair to match, he thought we were the stupidest bunch of idiots he'd seen in a long time. He listened patiently to the list of charges against us, then in his heavy Irish accent, he handed down the sentence.

"Let me tell you what I'm going to do, gentlemen. I will allow you to return to your rodeo to entertain the fine people of our fair city . . . providing, of course, that each of you is willing to make a little contribution toward your timely release."

Well, none of us expected to get sprung so quickly, and we were mighty grateful. Me and Lester went to emptying our pockets into Tom's hat. When we had the total amount of our "contribution," we handed it over to the big Irishman. I told him thank you, Tom and Lester waved good-bye, and the three of us high-tailed it back to the rodeo grounds.

We arrived in plenty of time for our events — sober, but real happy we weren't in jail. We all got good scores, and I even made a little money. So, we didn't feel too bad about our little excursion on the wagon.

For the rest of that night, and most of the next day, we behaved like perfect gentlemen — or at least the way we imagined gentlemen might behave. But after the rodeo the following day, Tom and me got to feeling restless again. We went to the bar for a drink, not because we were thirsty, but because we couldn't think of anything else to do. Or, maybe we didn't want to do anything else because it might get us in more trouble. Anyway, we were trying to decide whether to order a second drink when two sweet things shuffled into the bar and sat down at one of the tables.

Tom poked me with his elbow and whispered sort of low through the side of his mouth.

"Hey, Hoss, let's check those two fillies out. What do you say?"

We picked up our drinks and strolled over to introduce ourselves.

"Ooh . . . are you guys real live cowboys?"

203

"Well, we sure ain't dead," I said. "Want to pinch me and find out for sure?"

They giggled — which in cowboy language is the next thing to a proposal — so we sat down beside them. Tom started telling the blonde about Oklahoma and I let the redhead know I was from New Mexico.

"Oh! How do you like the United States?"

I couldn't believe what I was hearing. I asked her to repeat the question.

"Did you have to get a visa to come over here?"

I finally realized that she thought I was from Mexico. Tom started to speak up, but I beat him to it.

"We're not from Mexico originally. We moved down there a few years ago. We like it because the country is still wild and wide open — just like us."

Tom looked surprised, but he went right along with me. The blonde was curious, too.

"Please say something in Spanish," she begged.

I had learned enough to order a drink when I went to Mexico once. All cowboys knew how to do that because tequila was our main means of survival when we went south of the border. Except for that, I only knew a few cuss words. So, I just started rattling off those, added a burrito here, a peso there, and threw in an enchilada now and then for good measure. The others I just made up.

The girls cooed like a couple of doves. I thought the redhead was acting like she might fall in love, but the blonde was more interested in what I had said. She asked Tom to give her a translation. I was hoping, for his sake at least, that he'd come up with something special to say. That old boy was going to need some help if he planned to score with her. (Like I said, Tom was not a pretty hombre.)

He thought about it a minute and smiled.

"Well, Dan thinks you two are the most beautiful and charming senoritas he's ever met . . . and I say he knows what he's talking about."

The girls blushed and giggled some more, and Tom winked at me. I was biting my lip, trying hard not to laugh, when suddenly the redhead let out a gasp.

I looked up, and there stood two of the biggest, toughest old boys I had ever seen anywhere. One was all hairy and reminded me of a grizzly bear, and the other one looked like a mad grizzly bear. And five or six of their grizzly friends were standing right behind them.

"What do you cowboys think you're doing with our girlfriends?" the biggest bear growled.

Tom and me hadn't thought that far ahead. We had been so eager to make their acquaintance, we hadn't bothered to ask the girls if they were alone. When Tom looked around for a place to hide, I saw some other cowboys at the bar watching him and grinning. I recognized a couple of them. They were the ones that had called the cops when we were riding around the grounds with the wagon. I just knew they were betting that Tom wouldn't get out of this mess without getting his butt kicked. As for me . . . well, it had been a pretty good day so far, so I decided to take the bull by the horns. I stood up and took a deep breath.

"We're doing everything you ever wanted to do but never had the guts to try."

Then I rared back and popped him right on the chin.

That's all it took for the whole bar to explode. It was one big brawl — the bears against the cowboys — and everybody wanted a piece of the action.

Meanwhile, I realized that poppa bear hadn't even blinked. I thought, this is not a good sign. Somebody's liable to get hurt in a minute, and unless someone else moves into my boots real soon, it looks like it's going to be me. While he stood there waiting for me to make my next move, Tom was trying to recruit a few good men to help us out. But all our friends were too busy rearranging furniture, smashing bottles and glasses, and generally busting up everything that couldn't hit back. So, when I thought the big man wasn't expecting it, I took another swing at him. I got the same results — two, three times! Then it was his turn.

Wham!

He hit me so hard I just knew it was going to hurt clear into my next life.

This was one time I was glad to see the cops. On the other hand, these weekend rookies might as well have stayed at the donut shop. The first two dove right into the middle of the fight and nearly got themselves killed. The drunks were so fired up, they didn't even see the uniforms, let alone their badges. And when a third cop started spraying mace, those old boys just got madder. An Oklahoma cyclone couldn't have done any more damage. By the time the reinforcements got there, that bar was a total wreck.

The cops took a real dim view of getting whipped, but the most aggravating part was, they just couldn't explain what had happened. When the head honcho arrived — the same guy who had captured the wagon — the cowboys and the bears were all standing around comparing war wounds. In spite of their ripped shirts, busted lips and black eyes, they all were laughing and bragging about how much fun they were having.

The top cop gathered his troops and motioned for me and Tom to join them.

"Who the hell started this?" he looked directly at me. "And don't give me any cock-and-bull story about some hero trying to save the world. I'll bet you two had something to do with this little fracus. Am I right?"

There was no use denying it. Poppa bear hadn't forgiven me yet, and he just kept pointing in my direction until he got the cop's attention.

"Well now, that could be," I said meekly. "But we were just having a little fun. Everything was okay until those rent-a-cops started spraying mace. I figure they got what they deserve."

"They are an ignorant bunch," he muttered, drumming on his belt while he looked over the situation. "Tell me something. Are all cowboys nuts, or just you?"

"Neither. We just like to have a good time. Tonight we had a helluva good time."

Obviously, my loose teeth and bloody lip did not add up to his idea of a good time. I suppose he thought that blow to my head had impaired my judgment, and he was probably right. I smiled at him — just enough so it wouldn't hurt too bad — and he shrugged and went to rounding up the rest of my drunken buddies.

"All right, listen to me," he hollered. "You cowboys get out of here and don't come back. I'll recognize you if you ever do, and you can bet your boots, I'll lock every one of you up and throw away the key."

Nobody seemed to need a better invitation to get lost. We hauled ass out of there and never returned.

The rest of the rodeo was good to us, and for the

most part, we behaved like gentleman — with maybe one exception. That room at the Southside Hotel? Well, it probably had to undergo some renovations after we left, because that's where we did our partying. We all agreed we had had enough trouble with the law for one rodeo, and that cop had meant what he said. So, we stayed fairly quiet — and we stayed out of the bars.

Unfortunately, rodeos — like all good things — must come to an end. When the show was over, I caught the train back to New Mexico.

Compared to the ride north, the return trip was a disappointment. There weren't any Yankees on board — just a couple of Okies, and they were bigger liars than I was. I didn't attract a whole lot of attention, even though I spent most of my time in the bar. A few passengers glanced sideways at me. They all had painful expressions on their faces like any minute they might break down and cry. I guess I was a pathetic sight. My lip still hadn't healed up, and the swelling around my left eye had turned from black to purple and yellow.

When we pulled into the station, I gathered up my gear, jumped off that train, and headed right for the bar. Boy, was I glad to see Blink. I wanted to hear how that little colt was doing and, of course, him being there meant I had a ride home.

For once in Blink's life, that big red face of his turned white as milk.

"Hey Hoss, you are a sight! Are we at war with the Yankees yet? Should I go home and load my musket?"

At that point, nobody could have talked me into going back to Yankee Land . . . well, unless, just maybe, the South decided to rise again. But, like rodeos and all other good things, sooner or later a cowboy's crazy ideas all seem to come to an end, too.